At Leap of Faith Farm

At
Leap of Faith
Farm

Cheryl Suzanne Heide

Anamcara Press LLC

Published in 2026 by Anamcara Press LLC
Author © 2026 Cheryl Suzanne Heide
Interior art by Cheryl Heide
Cover art by Ellie Brockert Augsburger and Cheryl Heide
www.creativedigitalstudios.com
Author photo by Linda Hayes
Editor Vicki Julian
Book design by Maureen Carroll
Garamond, Gil Sans MT, and Aktiv Grotesk.
Printed in the United States of America.

Book Description: *At Leap of Faith Farm* explores the lives of the beloved creatures of Leap of Faith Farm.

ANAMCARA PRESS LLC
P.O. Box 442072, Lawrence, KS 66044
https://anamcara-press.com/

Ordering Information:
Quantity sales. Special discounts are available on quantity purchases by corporations, associations, and others. For details, contact the publisher at the address above.
Orders by U.S. trade bookstores and wholesalers. Please contact Ingram Distribution.

Heide, Cheryl Suzanne, Author
At Leap of Faith Farm

NAT016000 NATURE / Animals / Horses
BIO022000 BIOGRAPHY & AUTOBIOGRAPHY / Women
BIO030000 BIOGRAPHY & AUTOBIOGRAPHY / Environmentalists & Naturalists

ISBN-13: 978-1-960462-84-8 (Paperback)
Library of Congress Control Number: 2026935874

DEDICATION

—To my mom, dad, and sister who believed in me and encouraged my stories; my husband who lived the adventure and has always been my favorite reader; my friends in Great Plains Writers who inspired and kept me on task; and all the animals at Leap of Faith Farm who shared their lives with me.

Contents

PART 3: Heart Horses

Prologue:
A Lifelong Dream

It was a time of transition. After twenty years my husband and I were leaving our home in the western Twin Cities suburb of Maple Grove, our friends, and our jobs so that I could accept a new management position with the Minnesota Department of Natural Resources in southern Minnesota. Two years before, it looked as though our life together would end. My future husband and I struggled back from the rim of a chasm that threatened to swallow us. Now with hours of counseling behind us we took precarious steps toward not only a continued future together but also a new lifestyle in a new location.

It did not go smoothly. It was a turbulent series of months with no future job for my husband and no permanent home. Almost every weekend we made the two-hour trip south to search for my lifelong dream—a farm where I could keep my horses. Dick was not a city guy. Although he enjoyed my two horses, Dunny Money and Lars, and even rode with me occasionally, he was content to let someone else care for them. Living on a farm was not his dream, but he willingly went along with the effort to make me happy. The search for that farm was long. We were both getting tired of spending what little leisure time we had exploring deteriorated buildings, pastures with poor fencing, or land with no livable dwelling and winter approaching, a bad time to evaluate farms. Our Maple Grove house sold the week it was listed, and Dick took on the chore of supervising getting our home ready for a move and watching over our two cats Tasha and Smokey. As my new job got underway, I led a dual existence split between our home and my old planning position in St. Paul and motel rooms near New Ulm, my new job location.

Pressure increased as we faced the quickly approaching closing date for the sale of our home, and we appealed to our realtor to step up efforts to find us a new home. Finally, our weekend searches ended for a time. We didn't find our farm, but we did find a lakeshore home not too far from my work that we could lease for the winter. We were ready for a rest. We would look again in the spring.

In mid-winter, I made my last trip to our old home. With our leaving came the heart-breaking decision to say goodbye to our sweet Burmese cat Smokey who was dying from liver disease and had been hospitalized over the last few weeks. I carried the ghost of my dear boy and my guilt with me as we traveled away from our old life. With our remaining cat Tasha, a dwindling pet fish population, and most of our belongings locked in storage for an indeterminable length of time, we loaded critical items aboard a U-Haul and tearfully headed south. My horses remained boarded with a friend.

I was struggling with my new job and very busy getting to know my 300 staff members and traveling to visit the many offices across the vast region I supervised. My beloved and I argued over my work induced absences and his lack of work. I pined for my horses. Tasha missed Smokey and would not eat. We bribed her with midnight snacks resulting in habitual begging in years to come. We endured the Minnesota winter, watching beautiful sunsets over the frozen lake amidst someone else's furniture within a home we did not own in an isolated world.

In the spring we hiked by the lakeshore with Tasha. The sunshine was wonderful. I lay on the picnic table on the deck of our rented cottage and watched the sky turn bright blue overhead and listened to the drip, drip of ice melting all around me. At night, I often came home in tears, overwhelmed by the hostility and challenges that my position brought forth among the staff at my office. And we began our farm search again. Shortly after our move I found boarding for my horses and I trailered them south to a stable near our rental home. Our little family was all together in one place once more.

With the returning warmth, the lakeshore owner wanted his house back, and we moved again. This time student housing would be our solution—one of the few places that would allow Tasha and a short-term lease. All summer we lived in the depressing partial basement apartment, and even our explorations of the area and my time on horseback didn't alleviate our discouraged mood. Then, just when I felt we would be there forever, we found the farm. It was farther from work than I wanted, and farther from town, and bigger and more expensive than we had planned, but it was wonderful.

The house sat back from the highway a good two-thirds mile down a meandering gravel drive that offered glimpses of the river far below. White with terra cotta red trim, the house was impressive and charming. It was matched by a wonderful barn that could be made into a stable; a small woodshed filled with felled branches and logs; a huge shop; and a pole barn piled with cast-offs that almost hid the sand floor, masking its potential as an indoor arena. There was also a pond along with an apple orchard and pasture areas beneath towering craggy oaks. We agreed that much would have to be done there, and it cost way too much, but I looked around and envisioned my horses grazing within clean white fences and tucked at night into cozy stalls beneath a loft filled with sweet smelling hay. I imagined Tasha nestled between us, purring softly, as we sat gazing into the wood stove's embers, and I breathed out "Yes."

A shattered cup made the farm ours. The owner was just testing the market for potential buyers when her realtor friend persuaded her to show the house to us. She had operated the farm as a Bed and Breakfast called Cedar Knoll Farm. She called it a peaceable kingdom, and travelers, following the winding drive along the river to the door, found just that. Years before she had traveled to Minnesota from Philadelphia, leaving behind her position as a journalist with the city's newspaper and the home she shared with the husband she had recently lost. She later told us that while exploring the house prior to purchasing it, on the second-floor walkway she saw the ghost of her great-great uncle, a sea captain who had owned an inn. He told her the house was to be her home, and she should open it to travelers as lodging. The mystic quality that permeated the farm prevailed the day we visited. While gardening in the peony flower bed that arched along the drive, the owner had momentarily set down a favorite coffee mug, a gift from her family with a tiny red fox on the side like the foxes that frequented the farm. We felt bad when we learned that the realtor's tire had run over the cup, destroying it. But to the owner, it signified that the time had come for her to leave and we were the family she had been waiting to entrust with her farm. It was our destiny.

Part One: Our Stories

CHAPTER 1:
The Beginning

We moved into the farm gradually. We cleaned the barn first, making weekend treks from our apartment, until several years of dirt and debris and cobwebs and old hay were gone. Then, when we could finally believe that we officially owned this wondrous place, we left the apartment for the last time and became fully part of the farm and the future before us. We were married a month later on the sun porch under a drizzly dark sky that threatened worse with all our friends and family present. Still, we had a fairytale wedding that everyone loved.

And so we began again, at the farm we named "Leap of Faith" for all we had been through and how close we had come to losing it all, for the challenge of a new place and new careers, for the adventure of learning to be farm owners.

Learning the Ropes

I'd dreamed of having my own farm for so many years. It began when I was seven, I think, with shoebox stables for my magnificent Breyer scale model horses of assorted breeds and continued on a much larger scale to the roped-off sections of my parents' garage. In the Kansas winters of my childhood, while my father's pickup sat outside, its stall was occupied by my varied horse population—an elegant fiberglass palomino yard statue, a concrete burro, and horses I rode astride. My riding herd included a white mare with black mane and tail, and woven wire shoulder straps that allowed me to canter around our yard; a splintery black sawhorse with white yarn mane and tail; and my favorite, Stormy. His classic black head was mounted on a metal barrel perched precariously on top of my re-purposed and repainted Western Flyer wagon with a western saddle cinched so tightly on the barrel it would not slide when I put my foot in the stirrup to mount him.

I drew and painted all my dear horses' heads and sometimes entire horses without legs on fiberboard. Cardboard just wouldn't do for my steeds. Seeing there was no way to dissuade me from my love affair with horses, my father used saws to cut them free to attain their true horse form, creatively helping me assemble them, and even fashioning bridles for them out of leather scraps. Every night my horses, warm and cozy under sheets and blankets, waited in the garage for me to kiss them goodnight while snow blanketed the Ford outside.

Over the twenty-some years that I boarded my real-life horses, I studied how to take care of the wondrous and fragile beasts. Things I disagreed with in their management at boarding facilities, I promised to correct...if I had a place of my own. And all those years, my darling horses endured mismanaged stall conditions, dangerous wire, and treatment I could not supervise everyday so many miles from where I was living.

I died a little when my best horse-riding buddy sent a note to friends inviting them for a cookout at the new farm they had just purchased in another part of the state. "We bought the farm!" the note said. Another friend moved her horse to her farm as well. Meanwhile, my equine partners and I continued as boarders. I became good friends with the owners of some of my boarding locations and I trusted them explicitly with the care of my horses, but it wasn't the same as having them in my backyard.

My own farm seemed to be out of reach—floating out there somewhere, but impossible to find. Until I got a job that required a move to rural Minnesota. "Since we're moving anyway," I started the conversation with my husband, "can we at least consider moving to a farm?" He liked my horses, even went riding with me on occasion, but that is where his enthusiasm ended. Fortunately, he loved me. He wanted his horse-crazy wife to be happy. So, we looked for farms with 1.5 acres of grass per horse to graze, roads nearby to ride on, no open ponds, no toxic oak trees, and no dangerous wire fences. The list of "must haves" I'd assembled over my boarding years was endless. And it did seem to take forever to match my list, but then we found Leap of Faith Farm.

Dreams seldom match reality. I had never seriously considered all the aspects of horse management beyond my list of things I would change from my boarding days. Who tells you how hard it is to find good horse-quality hay? And who cautions you that road hay with its colorful array of beer cans, weeds, and pieces of metal and unidentifiable objects may interest horses but is not sustainable? My father insisted we make an offer on the field next to our property, that we expand our ten acres to twenty so we could grow our own hay instead of conducting yearly searches for clean palatable grass. He offered to help finance the land, but he disappointingly only gave us a business card from the local bank. Our landownership grew, but so did our mortgage.

We were fortunate to find neighbors savvy to hay production. They helped us select a seed mix of timothy and orchard grasses, and clover that the horses loved. And all the rest of our years at Leap of Faith, we rested easy knowing that the problem of having good safe hay was solved. Every summer, our neighbors cut hay for us, piling the sweet-smelling grass bales high atop their wagon. I admired their hay wisdom, knowing just when to cut, when to turn the hay and when to bale. We had our own hay, stored in our own loft, but a new worry emerged when I heard tales of barns catching fire and burning when bales of hay were put up too wet, causing fermentation and severe heat. My neighbors only laughed, telling us of lofts with hay so hot, you couldn't walk on the bales with bare feet. They suggested that if I was worried, I should just sprinkle salt in between the bales. I understood that salt would draw moisture from the bales, but the idea of restacking three hundred bales was overwhelming. Instead, for weeks following haying each year, I climbed the stairs into the loft, tested the changing temperature on my face, slipped my hand in between the stacks and crossed my fingers.

They never tell you how much manure a single horse can produce or how to dispose of the accumulating piles. We bought muck buckets and rakes and a shovel and worked to improve how quickly we could clean stalls and be on our way to work each day. We mucked out our stalls each morning adding barn lime to sweeten the ammonia smell, and pine shavings to offer comfortable beds. In good weather, when no crops grew in the fields around our farm, we spread manure from our stalls there each day using our little manure spreader. At other times, we composted it in a huge pile five feet high and twice that distance around. To spread the compost pile we relied twice yearly on our neighbors who arrived with their tractor pulling a "real" spreader. It was so nice to see the empty bare ground again after their visits, and hard to dump that first manure bucket on the ground again.

After my horse had serious accidents from single-strand wire fence, we opted for polyvinyl Centaur fence. An Ohio team from the fencing company quickly installed white wire and rails, crisscrossing our pastures and replacing decaying posts and rusted wire. It reminded me of the beautiful white fences of Kentucky where I worked before moving to Minnesota. And knowing I had created a safe outdoor enclosure for my guys justified the expense.

I had often selected feed for my horses at their various boarding homes, so finding the nutrients they needed was not a problem. Pasture management was another story. The horses had to be introduced slowly to the fresh green stuff in the spring even though they were practically jumping up and down in their eagerness to taste the horse candy. Sugars are very high in new grass and exposure has to be managed carefully to avoid serious illness. Once acclimated, the horses were in horse-heaven for the day until evening when we called them in for the night. It was a ritual we repeated throughout the season. Turnout was only the beginning pasture chore though. We rotated grazing across our two pastures and runs, mowing and then dragging to break up manure as soon as the horses were moved to another area. I always engaged in a mental battle with myself as summer turned into fall and then winter. It was so hard to take them away from something they loved so much. But my veterinarian pointed out it was the best thing for the pastures, removing my sharp-hoofed animals as the ground softened in order to save the plants for next year. How could I explain that to my equines? They would look at me with their great soft brown eyes and then stare at the gates, willing me to open them. But I was tough. "It's for your own good," I tried to reason with them.

They put grass restrictions right there with the other seemingly strange things their owner did. There were so many things I did to protect them. My barn no longer housed the horses of my childhood. They were real flesh and blood dreams come to life. I felt tremendous pressure to take care of them. On the farm there was no one to alert me to behavior that might indicate pain or illness. It was up to me to determine what it meant when a horse stood with his head in the corner or was unable to step up into the lean-to as they normally did, or left hay from the night before. I read constantly, always trying to stay one step ahead of the next problems. And my horses were no exception to the saying "If there is some way for a horse to get hurt, they will find it." I learned to take temperatures, soak inflamed feet, clean wounds, and give injections and medication. I constantly visited with my veterinarian and gained his respect while I gathered his wisdom.

Water freezes so much faster than we imagined in sub-zero Minnesota winters. The feed store helped us select a suitable deicer, or so we thought until one of my horses insisted on picking it out of the tank and throwing it on the ground. A built-in heater seemed to be an easy solution, but how many hours can one spend tightening and re-tightening a plug only to find the next morning, it had leaked and the tank had frozen to the ground? Buckets in stalls became four-gallon pop-cycles overnight. Our new morning ritual included hammering the outsides of each bucket until the whole ice cube fell on the ground to melt. God bless the person who invented electric buckets. Once plugged into an outlet, they kept water drinkable all night and a huge worry was removed from my worry list.

They were my horses. They trusted me to take care of them. I vowed I would not let them down. At night when I tucked them into their stalls and wished them good night, they looked deep into my soul and breathed their warm breath onto my hands, and I knew all was worthwhile. I was just where I dreamed I would be almost fifty years ago. The little girl and her horses had come home.

Adventure Road

Entering or leaving Leap of Faith Farm the river guided us. Our driveway followed the Big Cobb River's riparian twists and turns for two-thirds of a mile, its meandering pathway promising separateness and peace from the busy world at its threshold. And those who followed it to the end found a certain calm.

It was fall when the road first beckoned us to follow it. We drove along the gravel surface under a bright blue sky with rustling burnished gold corn stalks on one side, and the crimson and oranges of giant oak trees high above the river channel on the other. At the end of the road was a white house, glowing against the early autumn back drop with a terra cotta red roof overhead and a wonderful matching barn. We fell in love. We were home.

The driveway became a favorite walking path and horseback riding trail. It brought family and friends to our door. It welcomed us home from long days at work and rare vacations away. Down the driveway was a field road that skirted the edge of cropland, and then led down a steep grade to the river and other riding opportunities. In a world where every acre of land was treasured for its crop potential, finding places to ride was not easy. We depended on the generosity of our neighbors to allow us to enjoy the fields and woods on their cropland and Conservation Reserve Program land. So vast were the options for trail rides right outside our barn door that our horse trailer never left the garage except for transporting our horses for medical care.

Often on late summertime afternoons, clouds of dragon flies flew alongside our vehicles as we drove, an engaging escort to our home. Leaving our driveway and riding our horses up the hill into our hayfield in late summer, we disturbed bright black and orange Monarchs enjoying our prairie wildflowers. In the cool of summer evenings, before swarms of mosquitos drove us inside our sheltering house and barn, we walked our horses through magical firefly lights.

We delighted in summer and fall at the farm, but early winter and spring were more challenging times. And our driveway reflected the seasons. Late fall rains and early spring snowmelt changed the hard compressed gravel of the driveway to treacherous mud that tested four-wheel drive vehicles, and hard hooves struggled to gain foothold on the slippery surface.

Winter deserved our greatest respect. Gale force winds blew snow across miles of open fields, piling drifts high on the driveway. We layered coats, scarves and hats, put on boots and trudged through snow, sometimes over our knees, out to the barn to do chores, and then hurried back inside to observe the glory of a Minnesota winter storm. Cozy by our woodstove we watched the tree line across the field disappear entirely from view. As long as snow fell and the winds blew, we were captive. The drive was impassable until the snowplow operator we hired for the season could make his way through the drifted white. Often he would return several times each day to make sure we could safely get to the highway and on to our jobs, or for emergency trips to town for supplies, or sometimes freedom from our isolated world.

Plows pushed snow to both sides of the drive and created a new pathway for us to the barn and beyond for our horses. When the piles grew to the height of the snowplow cab, giant and powerful snowblowers were brought in to project cascades of snow further away into the fields. In the midst of the snow barrages, we played. I rode on the squeaking crushed snow surface down the road, the only trail not too deep for the horses. We took night walks down the snowy drive, the moon lighting our way, returning in a little while with numb faces eagerly seeking out the scent of burning wood and the iridescent glow from our house.

When the snow calmed, I rode up into our hay field. Wind sent the horses' manes flying, their hooves churning clumps of snow high in the air as I guided them in giant fox and geese circles or charged through deeper drifts. My husband and I sometimes strapped on cross country skis to transport us across the fields to the river. Our rawhide and wooden snowshoes offered a less tiring way of traversing deep drifts back and forth to the barn.

On one special occasion, New Years Eve, we traveled through the melted slush on our driveway into town for dinner and a movie after days of being stranded at home. We never imagined in those few hours away that temperatures would drop so severely. Now instead of forgiving slush, we faced frozen ruts. I tried to keep the tires on my Jeep centered on the highest parts of the frozen snow, but they slipped to the side and we were stuck. In our haste to escape from our snow prison we had neglected the Minnesota doctrine to always travel in the winter prepared for survival with warm boots and clothes.

Dressed in street shoes and a dress coat, my husband set out down the drive to bring help. I kept the engine running and waited, and waited. Finally in the distance I saw the welcome headlights of our little tractor coming to rescue me. I climbed aboard the tractor in my heels and evening clothes, abandoning the Jeep in its icy tracks. I held tightly to Dick, sitting on our shared seat, as we carefully made our way under the still full moon night back to safety and warmth. In the morning a neighbor came to drag the Jeep from its imprisonment. Once more our road, portal to adventure and home, was open.

We Just Wanted a Few Apples

Before we made the decision to purchase our farm, we strolled through the buildings and pastures, exploring. I spun verbal dreams to my husband of the potential that lay within the ten acres that would be part of it all. I envisioned my horses grazing within new white fencing, stalls cozy and warm with sweet fragrant hay in the loft high overhead, living in the instantly-at-home house with its tile floors, oak trim and wood-burning stove, and relaxing around what once had been a swimming pond that would need to be reclaimed from its overgrown state. What I had difficulty imagining was an orchard on our future farm. I knew horses and how they should be taken care of; I knew nothing about cultivation of apples.

The selling owner assured us we would love the orchard with its varieties of red and gold fruit, and truly enjoy harvesting the produce each fall and the many uses for the apples that were planted there. "A few trees should be fun," we agreed. "Going up to pick a few fresh apples now and then, and bringing apple treats to the horses sounds great!"

We soon discovered we were not talking about a few little trees here. The orchard encompassed at least an acre of land framed by our two pastures, the pond at the bottom of the hill, and thick woods which marked the outside border of the property. It had been planted to grass which unfortunately had been left unmowed and the thick blades tangled our feet as we climbed the hill to get a better idea of the entire landscape. There were a few little trees struggling to produce a few apples, and huge trees with gnarled branches that towered twenty feet overhead. So many trees! So many in fact that the owner had developed a diagram that would come with the property detailing the location of each tree and the kind of apples it produced—Delicious, Golden Delicious, Jonathans, Courtlands, Honeycrisps—all would be just steps away from our door. "Looks like a lot of work," my husband whispered in growling tones in my ear.

"So what do you do to take care of the orchard?" I asked the owner, hoping for a simple answer. "Nothing much," she replied. "The main thing is spraying early in the spring just as the flowers are falling from bloom to avoid scab, and then of course through the summer and into the fall to keep maggots from invading the fruit." Wow! we thought. Apples seemed to be as intensive a management challenge as horses. "I'm sure we'll figure it out and it won't be so hard," I assured my doubting spouse, unwilling to raise even the possibility of losing out on the wonderful farm because of a bunch of apple trees.

We purchased Leap of Faith Farm in the fall, too late to do anything to manage the orchard, so we contented ourselves with gathering apples as we wished, intent on beginning its care the following spring. We didn't count on how busy spring can be on a farm or the late spring freeze that sent white petals drifting like snow to cover the ground. We had watched carefully for the trees to bloom but we missed the pinkish white blossoms, the subsequent petal fall, and the opportunity to spray for scab.

Our apples, as lovely as they were initially, eventually developed bumps on their smooth skins. The previous owner had assured us that scab does not damage the fruit; it is just unsightly, so we forgave ourselves that year and every year after. We never sprayed for scab.

Spraying was a thing unto itself. We bought a sprayer to pull behind our mower and began caretaking our orchard. As the young apples emerged, my husband and I began our ritual spraying—one of us driving the mower from tree to tree and one of us applying the spray, appropriately coached by the other. I reasoned that we should concentrate on spraying the lower branches that we would most likely harvest. He concentrated on the "really good apples" high in the tree that could only be reached with an apple picking basket which we also purchased. Using the basket was fun, and it took some skill to capture the apples without them escaping and falling to the ground. Every spray time, which we repeated all summer long until just before harvest in the fall, was an opportunity to debate which apples were most important to spray.

We mowed the grass, an emerald carpet, that stretched beneath the trees. Apples that had fallen and were blemished or rotten were raked up routinely and dumped in the woods for wild creatures to enjoy in a futile attempt to lure them away from the trees. They loved to try the fresh fruit for ripeness. Apples frequently showed teeth marks or holes pecked into their flesh and then left behind. Clearing out the apples lessened the chance of disease spreading through the orchard. The one disease we could not eliminate was fire blight. It spread by contact from tree to tree, leaving dark cracked branches behind as though a fire had swept through.

The wonderful apples of Leap of Faith Farm were anticipated every fall. My family would come from Kansas for the harvest and take baskets and buckets of fruit home to enjoy. We would hold our breath as my elderly father, insisting on using the apple basket to capture the highest fruit, teetered beneath the trees stumbling over fallen apples on the ground while my mother and I were content to harvest the lower branches. Friends from work came each fall to join in apple picking, wagon rides, and a bonfire and cookout. We even set up a booth on the highway with a free will donation for any of our apples that passersby wanted.

We loved the apples, but even more we loved the orchard. It was such a truly peaceful place. Walking into the green meadow, seeing the trees with the wind blowing through the branches and the sunlight patterns on the ground, was magical. Often the cats would stroll along on our sojourn to gather apples, and the horses would stand watching in their nearby pasture waiting for a possible treat. We only wanted a few apples, but we gained a lifetime memory.

A River Runs through It

Southern Minnesota's landscape is a tapestry of golden corn and green soybean fields in the summer, and a dark vast plain in the fall and winter. Farmsteads are interspersed across the vegetative quilt, afterthoughts to the priority of the countryside. The farms float as islands on the ever-changing canvas, a small concession to the widely acclaimed fertile soil, some of the richest in the world—soil that farmers are reluctant to part with.

It hadn't always been that way. Early explorers like Joseph Nicollet recorded another kind of richness—a natural world with prairies of native grasses so tall a rider on horseback could lose their way. They found rivers winding through channels left by retreating glaciers, and a vast wetland complex that held soil on the land and preserved water resources. All these things offered habitat to animal and bird species never seen before and that have now disappeared.

Farming came to this rare environment, and grasslands were

forfeited first to iron plows, and later to earthen and then plastic drain tiles that diminished the wetlands to small, protected acres. Leap of Faith Farm was not exempt from the historic changes. Around our farm where our house, barn, pastures and orchard were located, were hundreds of acres of cultivated farmland. The Big Cobb River which half-encircled our property remained much as it had always been, though the quality of its waters was diminished. There were no longer any prairies or wetlands. The land no longer spoke to the human spirit. It spoke instead to different values.

When I came to Southern Minnesota as the Minnesota Department of Natural Resources Regional Director, part of my job was to help people understand the fragile relationship that had been compromised—how their plowed fields, the vanished prairies, and wetlands caused the rivers to carry soil and toxins in their rushing waters all the way to the Gulf of Mexico. I believed in my work, but I wasn't expecting to face the battle on my own land.

Our house and our barn were not built with water management in mind. They were constructed on the site of a post-Civil War homestead where once grasses and trees extended in all directions as far as the eye could see. There were no crops or bare fields. Our farm, located at the base of ten acres of tilled land was planted one year in soybeans and the next in corn, directly received the effect of rainfall and runoff. The slope of the fields seemed gentle enough when cornstalks and green plants hid the soil beneath, but during heavy rains across the bare land, water poured down the grade and then turned into a torrential current that flowed across our backyard between the pasture fence-line and the length of our house. It roared like a mountain stream into a small pond possibly constructed to absorb it all. The water cut deep trenches across our yard and eroded culverts and berms around the pond. An engineering nightmare resulted.

We tried to control the unmanageable water that was unleashed by constructing rock drainage ways along its path. We rebuilt berms and replaced culverts around the pond, hoping to restore its water retaining function but could never conquer the mighty water. I thought I knew about water management, but I couldn't apply it successfully in my own backyard. The solution to too much water too fast is always to keep the water on the land, slowing the flow naturally with vegetation that also filters nutrients and pesticides. The answer to our rushing stream was to buy the sloping ten acres of cropland that impacted our farm. The farmer who owned the land reluctantly agreed to sell us what he considered to be non-productive land.

In two years, the crop land became a field of timothy, clover, and orchard grass once again, except for the acre closest to our house. That acre was returned to native grasses and flowers. Where corn and soybeans and deeply plowed dark earth had been, now big blue stem, little blue stem, Indian grass, switch grass and a countless array of wildflowers bloomed. We refused to conquer the land, becoming friends with it instead.

Water always finds the easiest path in its journey. Although its flow through the field was tamed, it found another unfortunate route that demanded creative answers. I loved the curving white crushed gravel drive that we drove daily from the highway to our house and on to the barn. Rain was no problem; it was quickly absorbed by the grasses surrounding the drive. But ice was something entirely different, and rain on ice was a monster. Usually when winter came to Leap of Faith Farm it was there for the season. Snow did not fall and then melt away in a few days. It fell in layers, one on top of the next, daring the filtered sun to interfere.

On very rare occasions, the weather would warm enough to generate thunder-snows, pouring snow and rain down on frozen surfaces that had barely begun to thaw. The event resulted in dangerously slippery surfaces that caused us to hold our breath as we gingerly led our horses from the barn out onto safe surfaces and back in at the end of the day. We learned to make a narrow path of grit for them, just enough for their sharp hooves to gain traction through the snow crust.

We didn't anticipate that an overnight rain might channel water between the snowbanks on either side of the driveway down to our barn, and then inside it. In the morning, we opened the door to find standing slush down the barn aisle and into the horses' stalls. The enormity of the problem grew by the minute as temperatures began to fall and ice continued to form. We swept and scooped the icy debris out of every opening and by the end of the day, the floors were safe for our horses once again. "This cannot happen ever again," we pledged.

When spring came, we hired the contractor who had worked to channel the waters flooding through our backyard. He used the same system that the surrounding farmers had used to move water off their land. Drain tiles were installed around our barn that discharged to the pond, and in the lowest point in front of our barn, he installed a large rock-lined drainage basin. He completed the system by gently sloping the driveway toward the basin instead of the barn. We thought our barn was safe from future ice water catastrophes, but we still slept more soundly when we put sandbags on the floor inside our overhead door if there was any chance rain might fall on a frosty winter night. We felt secure with our solution until a thunder-snow event was forecast once again.

I braved the freezing rain and shone my flashlight into the drainage basin which seemed to be filling with water faster than it was draining out through the ice-covered drain. It might not flow into the barn I thought, but it was too big a chance to take. I carried the longest hose I could find out in the rainy darkness along with a little immersible pump we had purchased long ago. I placed the pump in the deepest part of the basin, connected the hose, held my breath and plugged in the pump. Though

I was doubtful, the little pump worked wonderfully, displacing water from the basin out into the paddock and another drainage basin placed strategically there as well. My horses slept warm and dry and no skating surface met my first tentative step into the barn the next morning.

The water that flowed across all the farmland around our farm ultimately joined the waters of the Cobb River. We loved the sound the river made tumbling along its way as we walked down our drive or rode beside it. The river, as it twisted and turned, caused steep bluffs to form across our farm. The river flowed far below our driveway, disappearing and coming into view through the branches of giant oak trees. We watched the river bluff drop-off creep closer to our driveway year after year, a driveway that had been constructed through an easement on land that we didn't own. When it became clear that the stability of the drive was threatened and we would eventually lose access to our home, we appealed to the previous owner of our farm who had retained the driveway easement. She arranged to have fill added to protect the driveway from further erosion and to shift the driveway alignment away from the river and further onto her easement. Valuable legal lessons and a better understanding of the complex nature of water and property rights were learned.

It Takes More Than a Riding Mower

We moved to our farm well equipped, we thought, to take on any management challenges that might come our way. The riding mower that seemed to gleefully clip the lawn at our suburban home in patterns with neat edges should be adequate for our country landscape. Maybe. And the powerful snow blower (the envy of our neighbors) that we purchased to clear the lovely but deep white stuff from our cul-de-sac drive would certainly keep our farm driveway clear and even sculpt a pathway to the barn on those snowy mornings before work. Wouldn't it?

"No!" was the answer to our naïve questions. We actually considered not purchasing the John Deere tractor, with its ominous loader and bucket suspended overhead, from the seller of our farm. She patiently advised us that the equipment she was offering to us as part of the farm purchase would be a wonderful asset. But, operating a mower and even a snow blower was something we had mastered. A tractor was an entirely different story.

Not detoured by our less than enthusiastic response, she invited us out to the shop for a quick demonstration. I quickly lost my way as she pushed levers, raised decks, lifted the loader high above us, and then rocked the bucket back and forth from scooping, to pushing, to dragging positions. And then there was the PTO (Power Take Off) lever that could raise and lower various attachments behind the tractor. "We'll never learn how to run this thing," I complained to my husband. He listened more carefully than I to her every word and seemed entranced with the idea of operating our very own tractor. In the end we became owners of the large complicated looking machine.

Things do turn out for the best sometimes. The tractor was amazing in its capability. Its sixty-inch deck cut easily through the lawn around our house and outbuildings and gamely took on the rough terrain of our pastures and orchard. It blazed trails through overgrown weeds and brambles that had not seen a blade in many years. In the winter we found the tractor much more reliable than our snow blower, which did not like gravel from our drive shooting through its chute with the snow and ended up spending its years at the farm housed snuggly in the shop. The loader pulled snow into manageable drifts and then scooped them aside creating walkable and drivable surfaces between the house and the barn as well and other outbuildings.

When we moved to Leap of Faith Farm, we immediately purchased manure forks, shovels, manure buckets, water buckets and other equipment from the Tractor Supply Company. One of our most treasured purchases was a large Rubbermaid wheelbarrow. It allowed us to carefully balance two and sometimes three manure buckets on top and push them all to the manure pile. In the winter a flat, black, plastic sled was used instead. It easily glided over the ice and snow to the pile carrying the same load, but steering and preventing the sled from sliding past us was a challenge.

We found that getting to the pile was only part of the work. Dumping was also a challenge, requiring some athletic ability and strength. Every day we climbed the steep pile as high as we could, dragging the nylon-handled manure bucket along. Reaching the summit, we tilted the bucket contents onto the pile and then slid back down to the ground, all while trying not to fall into the unstable stuff.

The piles were not allowed to stay in residence. They were instead composted at a grand scale until the neighboring farmers' fields were harvested and bare, and we were generously allowed to spread manure in them. Composting greatly reduced the amount of waste to be spread and broke it down as well. But composting required turning. I was grateful to put my shovel aside and transfer the job of turning our manure pile over to the green machine. With the loader lowered and the bucket parallel to the ground I would advance into the pile of bedding and waste and scoop up a bucketful. Lifting the load high above the pile, I slowly rotated the bucket and watched as the steaming contents came cascading back to the ground. Working a little one way or the other, I gradually made a complete circle of the pile until all of it had been completely turned.

Although our neighbors kindly agreed to spread the composted manure for us every spring and fall, we debated what to do about the in-between times. A manure spreader of our own was the obvious solution. Our Mill Creek spreader was a miniature version of the large, impressive spreader our neighbor drove into our yard twice each year. Approximately three and one-half feet wide by seven feet long, it was designed to be pulled by lighter weight machines and was a good match for our two-horse operation. To keep the pile at a manageable level from fall until spring planting, we dumped manure buckets into our spreader each day and spent the dawning mornings before work driving our tractor and the spreader across the barren fields. When snow made the fields inaccessible or seeding began the ritual of turning brown earth into beds for soybeans and corn, we turned back to the pile.

The riding mower we brought to the farm could mow our yard, but it took a long time, and it could not handle the rough terrain of our pastures. We turned to the nearby John Deere dealership for assistance. They were more than happy to take the ineffective machine off our hands and offer instead a small utility tractor. "Just take it for a spin around the parking lot," the dealer urged, and we fell in love with the quick, versatile, little machine. I didn't think we'd be a two-tractor family, but there we were. We maintained a close relationship with John Deere, who helped with the many little, and some large, repairs that having two tractors required.

Mowing was a major investment of time all summer long. With both tractors operating together, we were able to mow our entire yard in a little over two hours. The large tractor could mow each pasture and run in another hour. To keep our pastures in good condition and able to withstand the wear and tear caused by two horses, we practiced rotational grazing. We moved our horses from pasture to pasture at two to three-week intervals all summer long and dragged the pastures after each rotation with the flexible tine harrow we purchased. The tines on the interwoven metal device broke up manure piles exposing fly eggs to sun and air and greatly reducing the possibility of parasites being ingested into our horses' delicate gastrointestinal systems. Beyond being used to drag our pastures, the harrow was used for arena maintenance, turning the sand surface disturbed by sharp hooves back into a smooth plain once again.

Almost every clean-up or new project on the farm required transportation of things, equipment, and material. With no other option, the manure spreader was often pressed into duty, and I often rode along in the bed of the spreader behind my husband on the tractor, rather than walking the distance to the site. I knew there had to be a better solution and couldn't resist buying the little wagon that I found. It came as a kit consisting of wooden boards and bright red metal pieces. We were never a good do-it-yourself team, but we managed to follow the directions and ended up with a wagon that could easily haul things around the farm and unload with a tilting mechanism. With the wagon, we gathered, transported, and dumped branches and vegetation, and occasionally offered rides around the farm to family, friends and coworkers who joined us for hot dog roasts, with smores of course, and the opportunity to pick all the apples they wanted.

But picking apples required caring for them. We learned from the previous owner that meant spraying the trees and clearing out decaying apples from under each one. The clearing was a hands-on effort. The spraying was more puzzling until the John Deere dealer once again assured us they had the required equipment, and they would install a cable and plug on our little tractor to run it. A bright yellow tank about eighteen inches off the ground at its top and almost the exact width of the tractor came to the farm and was immediately put into service protecting our bright shining apples.

Killing weeds strangely became one of my favorite pastimes. I had been spraying the many weeds that constantly tried to invade our long, beautiful driveway and other inappropriate-for-weed places with a handheld pump, often riding behind my husband in the manure spreader. With our little yellow tank filled to the brim with the weed killer Round Up, the tractor, the sprayer, and I became a formidable trio in the war against weeds at Leap of Faith Farm.

My father just knew that we needed one more piece of equipment to round out our farm and brought us a Gator, a very handy and useful all terrain vehicle. Retired from schoolyard duty, the Gator traveled from Kansas to Minnesota in the back of my father's pickup. We didn't ask for the Gator, but this bright green John Deere machine became our favorite and most used piece of equipment. We eagerly awaited its descent from the pickup bed, down the never-used earthen ramp beside our shop. True to its name, the Gator went everywhere and was so much fun. It could pull the spreader and wagon with ease, carried us down the road to get the mail, and took us on adventures around the farm as well as on the surrounding gravel roads.

Every piece of equipment, once we used it, gained a respected place in our daily lives. Our friends from a nearby town loved to visit us to see how we were doing at Leap of Faith Farm. They lived on a large farm that had been passed down through generations, and the equipment they used to grow and harvest their produce was astounding. They always joked with me about the meticulous way I maintained my barn. "It's a barn!" they would say. "It's so clean in here, you could eat off the floor." Not really, I thought. Just my German heritage, I guessed, and the love of the land and growing things that I inherited from my farming grandparents, and great-grandparents. My friend jokingly referred to all our equipment as "toy" equipment. It was at a much-reduced scale in comparison to his farm, but it was not play. Too many things depended on us understanding that our chosen lifestyle took commitment and much more than we could have ever imagined. It took a lot more than our riding mower to make a success of Leap of Faith Farm.

What You Need Is a Sign

We knew what we'd name our farm even before we first found it—Leap of Faith. What else could it be to capture the upheaval in our lives? No one knew but us and the people who called, and missing us, received our voice mail message. "Hello, you've reached Dick and Cheryl at Leap of Faith Farm."

My father liked to fix things and always believed he had the solution to every problem, so it was not truly a surprise when on one of my parents' visits from Kansas to our farm, he brought along a sign. It was not just an ordinary sign, but a sign no one living in Minnesota would likely have ever seen.

I, as well as most Kansans, am familiar with the light-yellow limestone that predominates the landscape in western Kansas. Post rock was cut by early pioneers homesteading there to build fences and buildings in an environment where trees were almost nonexistent, and wooden structures could be swept away in prairie fires. The rock layer, which can easily be drilled and cut in straight horizontal lines, is often used to make yard signs. And now we fortunately would own one.

Finding the perfect place for the sign was easy. The curve of our drive as it entered our property was framed on one side by a huge stand of pampas grass, and on the other by a wild rose bed where a winged iron Pegasus sculpture flew. It would be the best location for the welcoming sign, we agreed. But that was the extent of our agreement. The "how to place it there" was another story. Making the sign part of the farm would not be an easy task.

Our tractor and loader found a new job, and we were glad to have our bright green machine. Just lifting the three pieces of stone that comprised the sign and its posts from the truck bed was a mechanical challenge. The weight of each stone was enormous, evidenced by the height my dad's pickup gained when its stone burden was removed. You could almost hear it sigh. Where were all the farmers who worked together to install a row of stone fence posts in pioneer days? It was just my father and husband with the tractor and heavy chains, and my mother and me cheering the project on.

How deep the holes for the posts should be was highly debated since they would have to be set deep enough to prevent frost heave, and yet digging holes by hand is grueling work. Finally, a "good enough" point was reached and focus shifted to how to get the posts into the holes. The posts with their ten inch by ten inch sides and six-foot lengths were not cooperative. They resisted chains being positioned beneath them and strained against the tug of the loader as my husband used his newly acquired tractor skills to swing them away from my dad's truck without damaging it and into position.

My father was the direction guy, indicating with hand gestures above the noise of the straining tractor: "Go left, no right, up a little, now down." He didn't deliver the directions from a safe distance to the side but insisted on standing his six-foot frame directly in front of (and often under) the loader bucket while Dick nerve-rackingly tried to comply with my father's hand signals. He lowered the bucket a few shuddering inches at a time, always mindful of my father's position and the ability of the tractor's hydraulics to hold the weight. My mother and I held our breath and then gasped cries of alarm as the bucket very nearly grazed my dad's head, or if he came close to stumbling into one of the post holes. But at last the posts were in place.

The final challenge was positioning the sign with our farm's name etched boldly into its surface onto the two posts. Signals intensified and tension escalated as the massive stone hovered over the posts and my father guided it onto stabilizing pegs with his outstretched and highly vulnerable hands.

"Leap Of Faith" the sign now told friends, family, and visitors that they had found our farm. And photos remain along with memories of the day: handshakes over the sign, Dick and me posing with our horses by the sign, my mom leaning over it smiling and happy the ordeal was over.

If Not for Neighbors

We heard the truck churning gravel down our long drive before we saw it. Eager to take a break from pulling the stubborn weeds that hid among the pink peonies along our drive, we awaited the identity of the rare visitor to our Leap of Faith Farm since moving there a month before. From behind the open cab door, a frothy-headed blond woman appeared. "Hi," she called. "I'm your neighbor across the field behind your barn. You can't see my place because of the hill. I'm looking for my dogs. Have you seen a lab and a setter? They got loose from their kennel." We shook our heads and introduced ourselves.

We discovered that in addition to dogs she had horses, a word that has unlocked the door to countless friendships over the years. In the coming years, we would rarely ride together, but I frequently rode across the field between us to the fence line that defined her farm. Once in view, I would call out her name.

Summer or bitter winter, if she heard my call she joined me, followed closely, her horses eager to visit mine. We all chatted together, enjoying the companionship for awhile. She and her husband sometimes joined us for dinner. It was during dinner at their home one night that we met their bright orange tabby Larena, who became our night visitor a few years later. Through them we became acquainted with other nearby neighbors and connected to people whose skills we needed.

We met another couple who lived just down the road. We had a very casual relationship, sometimes stopping by on a ride past their house, and it wasn't unusual to find the husband riding up our drive. He joked about his four-wheel drive vehicle that could carry him across all but the most deeply plowed fields. We would visit on the deck while his horse grazed nearby, and then as the sun gradually faded over the hills, he rode home.

Another couple, an easy ride down the highway from the entrance to our farm, raised Arabian horses and Golden Retrievers. Riding horses is always wonderful; riding with a friend is even better. She and I explored field roads and all-but-hidden trails that led to the Big Cobb River, creating our own pathways through the trees and prairie grass when there were none. When my horse Dun died, she brought flowers for me and a bouquet of carrots to nourish him on his journey away, understanding as only another horse person can, the devastation that comes from losing a being so great. She gave me a poem entitled "Don't Cry for the Horses" that resonated with the pain I felt, though my tears would not stop.

The Easter morning when Dun died, I didn't know where to begin to find someone to help prepare a resting place for my four-footed friend who lay quiet and still on the soft arena sand. It was the man who had recently installed our new septic system who came in the late morning with his tractor and backhoe to carry my friend through the apple trees in the orchard. A few years later when Lars crossed the rainbow bridge to frolic once again with his old friend, it was our snowplower who came quickly to help. It was hard to make the calls that would take my horses from my sight forever, but made easier by the quiet voices on the other end of the line saying only, "I'll be there" and then standing respectfully at a distance while I said goodbyes one last time.

The farm taught us that putting up hay is a science. It takes a farmer to read the weather in a way that will assure a rich, sweet smelling hay supply is there for hungry stock over the winter, instead of cut grass deteriorating in the field. My neighbors never called to tell me they were coming. I'd just look out the window and see their assemblage of equipment—a truck and a tractor pulling a hay wagon with a hay ladder tied on top—winding past on the way to the barn. Days before, we would hear them driving back and forth across the field, cutting the tall grasses. Several days later, after the cuttings had a chance to dry, they came again with their daisy wheel rake to pull the grass into windrows, low mounds of cut grass that are left to dry and then baled in neat rectangles for storage.

We all hoped for dry days and just a little dew to help with baling. Dick sometimes joined in loading the hay wagon, hoisting bales from the chute onto stacks on the wagon, and we both helped transfer the bales from the wagon to the loft sixteen feet above the ground. The hay ladder wasn't high enough to reach the loft doors. It had to be wedged and roped onto the bed of the hay wagon.

Belts and gears frequently broke and were pieced together, but every haying season our friends came to help. Our farmer friend and his muscular sons, and later their sons, showed up year after year to ensure we had a loft full of hay before winter. Dick and I took turns pulling a bale off the ladder before it hit the floor and then carrying or dragging it to a what would grow to a shoulder-high stack, wrestling it into position so the whole pile wouldn't fall, and then going back for another bale. My neighbors grabbed a bale in each hand and carried them to their destination, tossing them lightly into place on amazingly perfect stacks. Putting up hay reliably fell on the hottest summer day. By the time the last bale was in place and our dear neighbors had left for home, we emerged from the barn in dust-coated sweat and with very tired aching muscles. But I would look down the length of my barn at the stacks of sweet-smelling grass, imagine my horses contentedly munching on their hay as the winter winds and snow blew outside the cozy barn, and enjoy my own contentment.

The farmer and his boys helped us with other farm management as well. We tried to spread manure each day with our little manure spreader, but eventually crops grew in the fields or snow blanketed them and stockpiling became the only option. Just before winter and again in the spring, they came with their farm-size spreader and a tractor to load and spread the massive pile my horses had produced. A couple of loads and they were done. He and I stood watching as his sons worked, talking over the machine's roar. I listened carefully as he imparted that special knowledge, and sometimes folklore, that farmers live by and I learned to follow.

Not all our good neighbors lived nearby. As dedicated as we were to our animals, sometimes we had to be away for work or a rare vacation. People with animals on their farms don't travel very much, I learned. But for those times, we needed dependable help. Our neighbors were willing to assist in animal care occasionally, but they had animals of their own to manage, so I turned to Minnesota State University at Mankato and the students there. I never could have imagined that my advertisement looking for farm help would bring such an amazing array of students to our door. They came to work for us, one by one over the years, all eager to spend time feeding and playing with the cats, and grooming, feeding and occasionally maybe taking a ride on our horses. Some came to work for us only a short while, others for most of the time they were in college. Would-be police officers, teachers, nurses, veterinarians, engineers, scientists, artists—none could turn away from the magic word "horses."

They all seemed to love the time they spent at Leap of Faith Farm: the hours with the cats and horses, the respite it provided from the stress of campus life and school. We trained each of them to handle our horses safely. Some had been around horses all their lives, others learned horsemanship from us or through the equestrian classes offered at the university. Usually, chores were routine but sometimes they included administering medication, even insulin injections for our diabetic cats. Usually, we only needed help sometime during the day; sometimes we were gone for a day or two. The students provided us with the opportunity to leave the farm knowing our dear critters were in capable hands. We got to know our student caretakers very well, staying in communication long after they had graduated and moved on with their careers.

The veterinarians who we turned to when our animals were sick, or who helped us say farewell when they had to leave us, were a significant presence in our lives. Horse veterinarians are a varied lot. Our veterinarian in nearby Nicollet and the specialists at the University of Minnesota in St. Paul were treasured for their knowledge and willingness, and medical skill. Tall, rangy, and opinionated, my veterinarian at the Nicollet Veterinary Clinic always helped us find the right path for our horses, what was best for them. He dispensed praise and criticism with equal ease and always provided good information on any medical challenge our horses faced. He listened to our concerns, our worries as well as our ideas and thoughts about treatment, and spent time beyond his farm call, researching what might help. When Dun developed symptoms resembling a disease I had recently read about in a magazine, he searched for more information and agreed that Dun had Cushings Disease, a condition of the pituitary gland, now widely known and treated but almost unheard of at the time. He found a drug that could help with his symptoms. When my old boy started stumbling more frequently, it was my veterinarian who cautioned it was time to put aside Dun's saddle because he didn't want to hear I'd "taken a header off of him" if he fell. The day before my dear Dun died he was there making him as comfortable as possible and sharing in our grief.

My horses always seemed to be struck by diseases that veterinary medicine was only learning about. When Lars began looking unwell and then began exhibiting pain signs that didn't respond to treatment for colic, my veterinarian used a testing protocol he had just become aware of to confirm that Lars had an ulcer. And the next day when Lars was not able to travel for the emergency treatment he had arranged at the University of Iowa, my veterinarian responded to my frantic call for help and provided kind support when Lars left us.

When Nic mysteriously lost control of his hind legs during a lunging session and started bucking when he was ridden, my veterinarian ordered rest for my guy and then explored with us the possibility that he had contracted a devastating neurological disease. He later helped me find a trainer to work with after an accident with Nic that kept me from riding for almost a year. He steered us carefully through Raider's baffling laminitis and the treatment of, and eventual loss of, his beautiful soft brown eye, trying every possible way to save it. My veterinarian could always be counted on for good advice, good conversation and an unwavering interest in the welfare of our horses.

It took courage, patience, and kindness to treat the many semi tame and sometimes feral cats that came to Leap of Faith Farm. We brought them to the Minnesota Valley Pet Hospital in carriers we used to trap them, using enticing treats, or one time, a live trap. Never did the veterinarians object to examining or treating the half-wild creatures I brought to them. Even Jessie, who escaped from her carrier and raced around the exam room knocking items to the floor in her wake, did not discourage my veterinarian. One enterprising vet gradually subdued Jess by tossing a towel over her while she hid beneath the table and then waiting for Jess to calm down. Fourth of July weekend, the veterinarian on call responded quickly to my plea to help our Kasota who appeared despondent with a yellowing tint to his ears and eyes. His diagnosis saved Kasota's life. When our diabetic Chess's blood sugar levels fell and he entered a coma, and no one was available to keep watch over him, our veterinarian took him home with her, wrapped in a red blanket and kept vigil over our little cat until he was gone. Our veterinarians always seemed to understand the love we had for our animals and our willingness to do all we could for them, and often took extra measures and worked with us in their care.

There was a rag-tag assortment of farriers—horse shoers who kept our guys moving soundly across the land. "No hoof, no horse" was the common adage. Of various skill and attitude, they held one common attribute: they were all colorful figures. Some had little patience with my two fellows. They swore at them and were rewarded with swishing tails and stamping feet. Others made sure they always had a horse cookie that brought an affectionate nuzzle instead. Some were content to reshape shoes and reapply them until I requested new shoes be made. Others brought out the anvil and hammer every visit, measuring each angle and checking carefully before adding nails. One farrier competed across the Midwest in timed shoeing events; another offered to board both of my horses at his farm over the Christmas holidays when I could find no one to care for them. Farriers, like most people in the horse field, each believed their way was the best way. Like everyone else I met through my horses, I learned a great deal from each of them about horses and people.

The neighbor boy, across the road living with his grandparents, mowed our yard for our wedding and continued to mow for us when needed, particularly the steep slopes of our long driveway ditches. Many years later he purchased the land across from his grandparents' farm, beside the entrance to our drive, to build his own home. He kindly allowed us to continue to ride our horses down the field road behind his property to the river, and on the trails his family had created that wound through the woods and meandered along the riverbank. The neighbor who owned the land between our orchard and our neighbors' farm behind us, grew sweet dark-green watermelons that vined along the trail to our farm. He sometimes waved to us from his tractor as we rode by and invited us to pick a melon if we wished. On past his field a farm lane led to a gravel road, and at the end of the road was Conservation Reserve Program land owned by another farmer who granted us permission to wander his land on prairie and wooded trails. Thanks to our neighbors, every ride out the barn door had the potential for being an adventure.

Many others became interwoven with our lives at Leap of Faith Farm over the years. A contractor, who worked for my department addressing drainage issues, developed solutions to the many ongoing water issues we encountered on the farm—installing tile lines, reinforcing the dam around our pond, creating drainage basins and channeling water through drainage ways to avoid soil erosion on our property. The construction crew, who retrofitted our dairy barn into a wonderful stable, I discovered at the annual Horse Expo held each spring in the Twin Cities. They built stalls, a tack room, a storage area and an inside shelter for my boys. Another crew from Ohio took out rusting wire fence and metal posts, and installed in their place vinyl fencing, much more attractive and safe for horses as well. They weren't prepared for outside work in Minnesota winter when they arrived and immediately outfitted themselves with Carhartt overalls and jackets to withstand the cold. Their lack of familiarity with Minnesota's climate and the power of frost heave was evident many years after they left—the fence posts they installed pushed themselves out of the ground every spring. When the fencing was completed we hired a painter, who spent weeks painting each post white to ward off bored equine from gnawing on the wood during winter months, and who greatly enjoyed his relaxing lunches on the shaded tranquility of our deck.

Giant cottonwood, oak, and bass trees spread a canopy across our pastures. We were dismayed at the abundance of scattered limbs and sometimes whole trees fallen that resulted from a heavy thunderstorm, blizzard or ice storm. It was too much for our wagon and small chainsaw. "Better to call experts to manage the wood debris," we thought. The tree service arrived after each major event, sawing limbs, setting aside a stack for firewood, and feeding the remains through the wood chopper. They were a reliable resource for the challenges Mother Nature directed our way.

Everyone in every situation assembles people to help them manage their homes and their lives. It was the daunting scope of the twenty acres at Leap of Faith Farm with its many buildings, varied vegetation and animals that caused us to build the community of support we relied on so heavily. We were fortunate to be surrounded by kindness and the right people at the right time to help us. For all our neighbors, we were grateful.

CHAPTER 2:
Just Passing Through

Leap of Faith Farm was ours for just a short time—a place where many creatures traveled down the gravel drive to our peaceable kingdom or drifted from the constantly changing soybean and corn fields to find quiet solace. We never really possessed the rolling hillsides, or the river singing its soothing melody far below, or the wind whispering through the giant basswood trees. We were only another tenant, not the rightful owners. We saw ourselves as unintended invaders, bringing our human demands and activities into a world that existed long before we arrived. We tried to temper that by seeking harmony instead with those four-footed friends who came our way for a little while. But sadly, it could not always be so.

Delphinium Sacrifice

The previous owner had planted a three-tiered perennial flower bed, running behind the length of our house and stretching down a steep slope toward the pasture. I soon found I was not up to the task, in time or energy, to transform the now tangled mass of plants and trees and brush into the lovely display of diverse color and form the bed must have been when it was first planted. Instead, I hired a landscaper who set to work immediately helping me select plants that would add balance and charm to the garden. One of the plants she felt we had to have was delphiniums. I agreed, picturing the tall blue flowered stalks adding height to low-lying hostas and delicate coral bells.

The garden restoration was nearing completion as I went out one morning in late spring to stroll through the project before work when I encountered, not my lovely blue flowers, but empty stalks beaten to the ground. "What do you think happened?" I asked the landscaper later that day.

"Woodchucks," she stated flatly.

Possible, I thought. We knew they were around. We'd seen their engineered mounds and tunnels in our pasture and tried to keep up with new sites, filling them with dirt and rocks so our unwary horses would not step into a hole and possibly break a leg. As the horses spent more time in the pasture, the little varmints seemed to vacate it. Our theory was that they didn't like the thundering earthquakes that resulted from my boys playing chase across the pastures. But they didn't leave entirely. They loved to sun themselves on our deck, sitting their little rumps on the step and their forepaws on the deck itself, only stirring to stand upright on their haunches when something disturbed the normal quiet.

"My boyfriend can trap them for you if you want," the landscaper offered.

It had been an expensive project, and my glorious delphiniums were a highlighted item on the bill. I agreed to the capture. But not to the means or the aftermath. Live trapping, I assumed—not the terrible end to the woodchuck I discovered the next day when the boyfriend checked his trap. Instead of finding the woodchuck secured in a trap awaiting transportation to a new location, I was horrified to discover he had beaten the poor woodchuck who only had an unfortunate taste for my flowers.

I thought it couldn't be worse until the next morning when I once again toured the garden and discovered three little furry balls on the lawn, looking for their mother. How could the man so cruelly kill an obvious mother woodchuck? I made a call to the landscaper once again. She apologized for her boyfriend's action and asked what she could do to help. We picked up a powdered formula, tiny kitten bottles, blankets, and a box. We hung a heat light overhead for warmth and took turns over the next few days feeding the tiny babies. I still can see their little paws, like little hands holding onto the bottles and our fingers.

In the end, they all died. I have never trapped another wild being. And there were never delphiniums in my garden.

A Long Haul

"Come in and see what I found in the back of the barn," Dick called to me on a warm summer afternoon. It was steamy, made more so by the recent rain that had fallen, a storm lasting several days and now humidity had taken its place. In the back of the barn, hiding in a dry dark corner was a huge turtle. "I think he must have come up from the river," my husband said. "What do you think we should do with him?" I asked. "He needs to go back to the river." Easy statement, difficult to make happen. The turtle was massive and demonstrated a reluctance to be disturbed by arching his neck in all directions and attempting to snap out at whoever happened to be in his reach. There was no way to pick up the struggling amphibian, except maybe a shovel. It took some doing to maneuver the pie-plate size guy onto our reliable barn shovel and keep him there. And then there was still the matter of a transport vehicle. We settled upon our wheelbarrow. Every day we used it to haul muck buckets full of manure to the pile and it was deep enough he probably couldn't climb out.

With a little effort, the turtle was lifted and slid off into the wheelbarrow for his riverside ride. Off went my husband across the field and down the root-laced trail to the river. He finally came back with all fingers intact though he explained it was touch and go as the turtle continued to snap at every opportunity. It was a very determined turtle, but an equally determined husband prevailed.

Opossum Roundup

The enticing scent of cat food drifted down the loft stairs beckoning our tribe of barn cats to halt their roam through the corn stalks and rich green soybeans and join the feast. We fed them twice daily, just before chores and again when we shut off the lights and made our way to the house for our own meal at night. In the winter and in other seasons when temperatures allowed, we closed the barn for the night, carefully counting noses to make sure everyone was safely inside. But during muggy Minnesota summertime nights, we left the big barn door open to maximize air circulation for the horses and our feline residents. Food was left out for casual dining throughout the night. We never imagined the dilemma that leaving cat food available would cause, but we quickly learned that it was especially appealing to opossums and raccoons as well as the many mice that scampered throughout the barn. The prehistoric, interesting but non-cuddly, opossums claimed remaining food as their rightful trophy. As our cats gazed on from their cozy hay bale beds, time and again one of the daring beasts ascended the stairs and crunched contentedly away, unless by their misfortune, we discovered them. They were territorial about their claim, looking down their pointed pink noses at us with their dark beaded eyes, sometimes hissing at us in warning.

Not ones to just accept defeat without a fight, Dick and I devised what we proudly called an opossum roundup. The event happened so frequently we became quite good at it, could have even recommended it to others. Equipment included a broom and a plastic trash can with an essential lid.

Once the rascal opossum was spied, one of us would station ourselves at one end of the barn loft while the other held the trash can on its side at the opposite end. And then the games began. The broom handler swept the broom toward the critter, who did not take kindly to our suggestion that they move away from the cat food dishes. Fortunately, a prodding broom provided good incentive to vacate their position. The challenge was to keep the opossum momentum going down the length of the barn, a task much simpler when the aisle was clear without stacks of hay to hide in. If our hockey sweeping strategy was derailed by the furry puck diving into a bale, the game had to stop until he could be poked enough to move forward again.

The dark hole provided by the tilted can always proved hard for the opossum to resist as he tired of being guided left and right down the aisle. Once inside, the can handler quickly set the can upright and secured the lid. Then it was down the stairs and into the back of the pickup for what was always a dark night trip down to the canoe landing a few minutes away. The can was lifted out, tilted once again on its side and the lid was removed. The opossum was encouraged to leave his slippery plastic den and we watched as he waddled away in the truck headlights into the woods to begin another life.

Opossum relocation was an art we had not planned on. We worried about the little guys, but much less than we worried about the disease that they frequently carried that could be transmitted to our horses with devastating neurological consequences. Eventually we became wiser and began feeding our increasingly gentle cats in the chicken coop kennel tucked under the stairs. We picked up the cat food more frequently, added screens on our barn for ventilation, and the opossum became just another fascinating creature we welcomed and observed from afar at Leap of Faith Farm.

In a Tree Trunk

Raccoons occasionally found the flavorful cat food too much to resist. We didn't often find them at the food bowls in the loft, but we saw them frequently around the farm. Perhaps they were more reluctant to risk the climb up the stairs or were not able to overcome their fear of humans. I was surprised one winter evening, then, to see not an opossum's rat tale disappearing around the hay bales in the loft, but a black and gray striped one.

I doubted that the opossum trapping method would work with this guy; an element of surprise and chase seemed more effective. I sat quietly among the hay bales and eventually a large raccoon came rambling out and crept toward the cat food bowls. I waited until he was near and then moved quickly forward, broom in hand with a hearty "Get out of here!" yell for good measure.

He was surprised and did begin to run, but he seemed disoriented, unable to find the stairs that he had climbed. I directed him toward the top step. He went over the edge and began clumsily descending them one at a time. Then in horror I watched as the little invader fell, tumbling down one flight and then the next to the floor below. I followed his fall, feeling terrible that I had caused the poor racoon's unforeseen accident. Why had he fallen I wondered? What was wrong? He had seemed to move normally along the loft floor, so his legs were working fine.

I stood at the bottom beside the poor raccoon. He appeared to have recovered from his fall and was now backed against the wall downstairs, growling a warning to stay back. In the better light of the barn aisle, I could see him more clearly. Eyes that should have been shiny black in the light had a blue film across them. He was blind. Guilt rose quickly within my heart. He could not see the stairs and in fleeing for his life he had lost his balance and fallen. I thought how old he must be. Perhaps hunger and his inability to find food had motivated him to overcome his instinct to stay away from buildings. The appeal of cat food was just too much to deny.

I opened the front door wide and stood back watching as he ambled slowly out into the night. The fact that nothing seemed broken didn't lessen my concern. Minnesota winters can be brutal and I feared for him in the cold, blind and now maybe injured as well. Our old woodshed just a few feet from the barn would provide good and safe shelter, if he could find his way inside, but there was no way to ensure that would happen.

There were many little raccoon hand prints visible with each new snow throughout the winter, but I never saw the blind raccoon again. I didn't want to think about what happened to him.

Spring came and we began cleanup around Leap of Faith Farm. Behind the woodshed, the old willow tree had shed many branches, and we spent one brisk sunny day picking them up so we could begin mowing. I found myself on the south side of the tree, away from the barn studying the old tree and its gnarled trunk. At the base of a wide fork, I found a large cavity I hadn't noticed before. It was low enough that, standing on my tiptoes, I could peer inside. Deep in the darkness, I could just make out the bleached white sculpture—the bones of what was most probably the old raccoon. Tucked away, so terribly alone, all the long cold winter.

Ghost Deer

Wild turkeys, owls, bald eagles, squirrels, rabbits, and coyotes lived in the woods and fields around Leap of Faith Farm. We saw them frequently, marveling at the wildlife that were part of our world every day. But it was the deer that moved so silently around us who thrilled us with their mystical appearance. As magical as we found them to be, the deer's silent approach never failed to frighten the horses. Each time it was as though they had never before seen the strange beings with four legs that moved differently than other horses and smelled nothing like them. On a blissful morning's amble to the pasture, an unexpected encounter with a small fawn at the end of the run once caused my red, seventeen-hands tall horse to screech to a halt, snort loudly, whirl away and race back to the safety of the barn. Other times they grazed peacefully close to each other, separated only by the white vinyl-encased wire of our fence.

The deer frequently drifted through our yard, sampling choice grass blades beneath the clothesline, browsing the impatiens we placed high off the ground on top of an old wooden barrel. They kept distant from us, watching with great round brown eyes as we worked around them. Many times I tried to get close to them using the natural horsemanship training that I successfully practiced with my equines. I walked quietly toward them, relaxed, my head down, my eyes downcast, watching from the corner of my eye, alert to the slightest sign of movement. When they began to move, I retreated and advanced slowly again, sometimes getting to within twenty feet, sometimes closer. Then a white-edged tail would flag danger, a lifted forefoot would signal a desire to flee, and they would bound away through the green and yellow soybeans or leap across the deep furrows of dark rich plowed fields.

Leap of Faith Farm was a favored refuge for individual bucks with proudly displayed antlers, does with young fawns at their sides, and entire roaming herds. It was ideal habitat with the soybeans and corn growing on vast acreage, woods that offered year-round shelter, and the Cobb River always providing fresh water.

We carefully mowed our pastures in the spring and summer months, always on the lookout for tiny fawns that hid in the tall grass as their mothers directed. Standing barely a foot tall, they remained where she led them. Sometimes barely escaping our tractor, they waited till danger was upon them before darting away, a current through the grass, the only evidence of their narrow escape. No fawns were ever injured on the farm, but our farmer neighbors told horrific tales of babies being caught up in combines during soybean harvests.

Still, one deer might have been injured by our actions. Heading up into the pasture on our tractor to mow one summer day, we startled a youngster who fled with his companions. Unfortunately, he was watching the approaching mechanical monster so intently that he ran into one of the giant basswood trees that towered above our pasture grasses. A cartoon figure of a deer, his forelegs wrapped around the huge tree trunk before he fell back, shook his head and seeming unfazed, pranced away with his herd. I wondered if perhaps he was blind, puzzled how the basswood could not be seen, and hoped the little deer would be all right.

The deer came in all seasons, but they especially favored the fall when apples in our orchard turned ripe and the scent of apple juice filled the air. We tried to keep up with harvesting the plentiful apples—Jonathans, Red and Golden Delicious, and Minnesota favored Honey Crisp. Still, great piles of fallen fruit scattered beneath the trees, an invitation to all wildlife to enjoy the harvest as well.

In early winter, our orchard and pastures became a haven from orange clad invaders and blazing gunfire that surrounded Leap of Faith Farm. We did not hunt and posted our land with no trespassing and no hunting signs to enforce the security our farm provided. Hunters hovered around all sides though, getting close enough we could make out their features. My horse Lars, forever protective of our property, watched them from the dry lot. He warned them to stay away, nodding his head and pawing the ground. Still they came.

We brought our horses close to the barn, confining them in small paddocks and runs throughout hunting season. It was not unheard of for hunters to mistake horses and cattle for trophy bucks. We always feared our pasture restrictions, the orange ribbons we tied in our horses' tails, and the orange safety vests we wore when riding out would not be enough protection. We kept the horses safe, but the deer were so vulnerable. Even with the protective haven we offered, on more than one occasion hunters drove into our yard requesting that we allow them to retrieve a "harvested" deer that had fled onto our land.

As winter approached, the deer became almost invisible against the dormant brown grasses and leafless trees of our pastures, having long shed their reddish summer coats for their camouflaged grayish brown winter ones. They often congregated along the fence line on the downward slope of the pasture, seeking shelter from approaching storms and the wintry winds that howled through the trees.

On a winter evening, when the setting sun spread a rose glow across our pasture and first snowflakes began drifting through the tree branches, they came softly, ghost deer disturbing not even the air in their descent. Settling among the trees, they folded long legs and lay down in warm seclusion. Snow, not yet the storm that would come later, gently covered them, insulation from the cold and danger around them. The ghost deer rested in such peace that just watching them, our hearts grew quiet as well.

A Creature Was Stirring

I've loved the poem "The Night Before Christmas" since I was a little girl. I could recite it from memory at age five my mother said. One of my favorite images is of sweet little mice with soft gray fur and pink ears, snuggling into warm nests as snowflakes dance past the window.

I wasn't prepared for the real-life mice that not only snuggled into our house at Christmas, but on every other day we lived in our Cape Cod home at Leap of Faith Farm. They were cute, but they were destructive as well. We didn't have mice in our house near downtown Minneapolis or even in our home on a quiet cul-de-sac in one of the Twin Cities' most western suburbs. But our true country residence found us with much stirring on the part of the little rodents.

The stirring of our house-mouse population, however, couldn't compare to the rats that had invaded the grain bins left behind by the previous owner. We didn't want grain bins; we wanted more grass corridors for our horses to roam but finding them a new home was a daunting chore. Three of the giant metal structures sat on concrete pads between our garage and our pole barn. We patiently mowed and trimmed around them for several years before deciding they had to go. Advertising that we had three grain bins in excellent condition seemed easy enough, and we were rewarded with a gentleman who came right away to look at them and to offer us a price. Naturally enough, he wanted to look inside before making an offer. We had never really bothered to pull the doors open and look inside. We had no reason. But he did. He pried the clasp off one of the bins and lifted his foot to climb inside just before he slammed the door shut exclaiming, "Its alive in there." When he could calm himself enough to speak, he told us that rats were everywhere inside the bin. He was interested in the bins, but we would have to make sure the rats were no longer in residence before he would purchase them.

We had no idea how to displace a bin full of rats, but the clerk at the local Tractor Supply Company immediately had an answer. Rat poison was the key, he said. "Just fill up some bowls with a little of the stuff. The rats will get thirsty, take a little drink, and that will do the trick." We hated the idea of a mass rat execution, but we didn't want rats to continue to be part of the wildlife at the farm, and we wanted to sell the bins. Within days, there were no rats inside. The farmer hauled away the bins, we hired someone to break apart and take away the concrete foundations, and we planted grass seed where little rat feet had run.

Most people who live in the country have mice. We were no exception. Our house sat in the midst of soybean and corn fields along a river with woods surrounding it all. We were intruders in their habitat, so of course they felt they had a right to be inside, particularly in the fall when temperatures dropped and the little creatures knew winter was coming close behind. They were not obvious to us, but our cats were aware of their presence. Every now and then we could hear our kittens' claws scritching across the tile in pursuit of likely mouse prey. When we caught one of our felines in the very obvious act, with a mouse tail and back feet hanging between their teeth, we would whisk them away to the nearest door. Holding tight so our kitty would not escape with the mouse, we gently pried their jaws open saying in a stern voice, "Drop it, drop it!" until they complied, and the mouse ran out into the night.

Other captures escaped our rescue attempts. That is when we would find little mouse masks on our tile or carpeted floors. All other traces of the mice were gone. Only their eyes, nose, mouth and whiskers remained. It was precise surgical skill on the part of our cats, and severe misfortune for any mouse.

Part Two: Our Winged and Four-footed Friends

CHAPTER 3:
Wiley—Forgotten but Not Gone

The first time we heard him crow, we thought banshees were stalking our barn. But the sound came instead from a scrawny, elderly, bantam rooster. He was the sole survivor of the animals that the previous owner had kept at her Cedar Knoll Farm to entertain guests who came to experience a working farm bed and breakfast. All the other animals were sold several years before to neighbors, including a flock of chickens. Our sly rooster had eluded the buyers, probably hiding high overhead on the rails of the front barn door. That's where we first spotted him, perched over our heads amidst the dust and cobwebs, tilting his head from side to side to examine us carefully with each yellow eye.

We asked the owner if she knew one of her livestock remained and what she wanted to do with him. At first, she denied the fact that there could have been one of her chickens living in the barn for so long without her knowing it. We agreed it was surprising. What had the poor thing lived on for so long? Where had he found water? How had he escaped capture by predators? All were questions only he could answer, and he remained resolutely reserved from his 13-foot perch. Not a friendly bird we judged, but who could fault him? Not friendly, but very clever. "He goes with the farm," his owner announced. No, we argued, we were horse owners, cat owners, not chicken owners; we knew nothing about chickens and couldn't roosters be very aggressive? Not her worry, she affirmed. So, he became ours.

We thought Wiley was a beautiful chicken with his ebony feathers touched by iridescent green, blending upward into copper around his head and neck, and highlighted by a brilliant red comb. We bought chicken food, put out a bowl of water for him and hoped that someday he would decide it was safe to descend from above us and let us approach him. And gradually he did. Still, it would be many days before he was comfortable in our presence. The little rooster would on rare occasions venture very hesitantly from the safety of the barn and up into the yard nearer to the house. We encouraged his forays by placing tempting grain there. Soon he would come to peck across the vast space between the two buildings. He never stayed long though, and he always left in a hurry. At the least startling sound, he would stretch out his neck, fold back his wings and skitter across the lawn, not stopping until he was safely enfolded in the barn's quiet darkness.

It was his shrewd approach to life that led my mother, on one of her visits from Kansas, to name our rooster. "His name should be Wiley," she said and so it was. Dear Wiley, our remarkable bird. So many things he would teach us, including how to love a rooster.

Not long after we moved to our farm, we began the arduous task of readying it for our horses. We hired a barn retrofitting firm from the Twin Cities, and they began transforming our old structure with new stalls and an inside lean-to. Daily they traveled to Leap of Faith and worked the wood they brought with them into a home for our ponies. Their sawing and sanding left piles of fresh shaving on the floor that proved the attraction we had been seeking to lure our elusive rooster down from his overhead perch. He pecked his way through real and imagined bugs among the shavings, and then fluffing his feathers and moving bits of wood and dust here and there, he created a perfect nest. He sat there amidst the whine of saws and shuffling of steel-toed boots.

The work crew adopted him as their mascot, a stubby feathered companion that oversaw the construction in our absence. They talked to us of his escapades through the construction debris and of his love for French fries from their noon meals. After years of isolation, Wiley was surrounded by people and their noise and laughter. Every day brought another tale of what our rooster had done.

Fall faded soon to winter that first year on the farm. The chill was unmistakable as I hurried off to work each morning, and Dick began his daily ritual of ridding our farm of the debris and waste it had inherited over the years. Two semi-trailer size trash containers were deposited empty in front of our barn, and then recovered weeks later, filled to overflowing. And underneath it all, an indoor arena emerged while an outdoor arena took the place of deteriorating hog barns. Grass grew beneath the thistles and burdock that intertwined among collapsing wooden feeders where no animal would ever eat again. On weekends and evenings in the fading light, we tore apart and deposited the castoffs that typically accumulate on farms under the out-of-sight, out-of-mind philosophy that had left Wiley neglected for so long.

In late fall we brought our horses home, and Wiley, for the first time in years, had farm companions once more. With new importance he supervised our morning and evening chores. Atop the stalls he would watch with fascination as we cleaned them, shifting through shavings, removing manure and wet spots, and making more wonderful nesting areas for him and soft beds for the horses.

Unannounced and with no apparent stimulation he would suddenly throw back his head and crow a loud screeching sound that drowned out the background radio and eliminated any chance of carrying on conversation. He crowed in the morning with the rising sun and at night in the surrounding darkness, so enthralled was he with his ability to emit a sound no other creature could mimic. He startled the horses at first. They threw their heads up wild-eyed from their grain, ears pricked forward, nostrils flaring. Then realizing it was "Oh, just a bird," they immersed their noses deep into the hay once again.

Hay was in Wiley's barn once again. Not the dusty moldy stuff he had lived with for years, but fresh green fragrant hay bales stacked neatly in piles along the length of the barn. At night he climbed the stairs to nest in the soft hay bales, descending again in the morning for a drink of cool fresh water and chicken feed in the little metal pan we had purchased just for him.

When snow fell that first year, we worried about our lone chicken with no other chickens to roost with for warmth. We invested in a heat light for Wiley. We carefully weighed the dangers of fire with the comfort of our charge, and Wiley's welfare won out. Since he already seemed to be altering his patterns to spending time in the evenings on the roof of the tack room next to Lar's stall, that location was selected for the light. We tied it securely to the beams overhead. When he discovered the joy of heat radiating over his chilled body, he quickly became attached to the warming light and perched himself beneath it on the edge of the tack room frame. "Poor rooster," we lamented, "he needs a nest to cozy into." So, under the light we placed a small rubber tub filled with shavings and shredded corn husk bedding. He was skeptical at first, distrustful of this additional creature comfort, but not for long. Curious to see if he was becoming accustomed to the new furnishings, we looked up with concern to the tack room roof. We didn't see our Wiley at first, but then we saw him under the light, deep in his bed with only his red comb and tail feathers showing over the edge. Other nights he was content to sit on the edge of the tub, spreading his feathers to absorb the soothing heat, a thin stream of vapor trailing from his beak illuminated in the glow.

Our barn was not predator-proof. We opened doors and windows whenever we could for ventilation, so wildlife occasionally entered the barn undetected and hid in the dark recesses of the loft. Knowing this we engaged in a nightly Wiley round-up. After eating and then taking a long cool drink from his water dish, Wiley would stroll—or more accurately strut—casually up and down the barn aisle while we prepared our horses' stalls for the night. Our last chore was to herd Wiley down the barn aisle to the half-door that separated a storage area at the back of the barn and served as a launching spot to his bed over the tack room. Slowing, arms outstretched, we moved our bird closer to his resting spot. He did not like this enforced nesting and took every opportunity to double back, ducking beneath our arms and racing back down the aisle where we began the process once again. He clucked and chattered the whole way, finally flapping his wings and rising first to the top of the door and then to his nest. "Good night, Wiley" were our closing words each night before we turned off the lights and headed to the house.

We had wonderful light in our barn; windows flowed along each wall, letting in the outside light and frequently the sun. It shown into the stalls turning the wood and shavings into a warm gold. Wiley discovered the fact that the sun and bedding made an ideal dust bath spot. He arranged bits of bedding into discreet locations that only he could detect, sneezing occasionally from the dust he inhaled; then he rolled in the softness, lying first on one side and then the other until each was exposed to the rays. We saw him lying there, neck stretched forward, legs to one side and were convinced he was dying. But no, he was very alive and sensing imminent capture, quickly scurried between our legs and out the door.

As friendly as he became, he was very much a rooster. He did not allow petting so I resisted when our farrier, after trimming the horses one visit, commented that Wiley's beak needed trimming and offered his assistance. "You'll never catch him," I warned. The farrier, though, continued talking about the horses and the weather as he moved closer to our bird perched on the stall watching. So quick, neither of us saw it coming, his hand streaked forward and grasped Wiley's legs in a single seamless sweep. He lifted Wiley, wings flapping and beak stretched wide in a screech, from his perch and handed him to me. I held my rooster for the first time, surprised how light he was, nothing but bone and feathers. Then I watched amazed as the farrier brought his trimming tool forward—not a small clipper that matched the scope of his task, but large metal hoof trimmers. And yet he was so cautious with them, the tools of his trade, that I breathed a sigh as did Wiley. In seconds, the eagle beak was gone, replaced by a chicken-sized appendage. He also carefully trimmed off the spurs that had grown so long they interfered with movement. Stroking his russet wings once more, I released our captive who flew to the safety of his nest.

Running a farm is a learning experience; you change your work and how you do things as problems are encountered and new solutions are found. We first cleaned our stalls at night when we had more time than the hour or so before work each morning allowed, but Wiley helped us change our program. We discovered that the horses' manure, instead of being in neat orderly piles, easy to sweep up in a single fork swipe, grew to resemble confetti over the day. "How did this happen?" we wondered, concerned about parasites and our horses' diets. That was until we observed our bird's nasty habit of picking through the piles for bits of feed. Disgusted, we changed our chore schedule so only clean stalls were available to him each day. Though manure picking was discouraged, we marveled at and applauded his keen ability for insect harvests. Wiley could pick up a grasshopper in mid leap from the concrete floor in the barn. He patrolled the yard around the barn daily, removing all creeping creatures he found with great efficiency.

It seemed Wiley would always be part of Leap of Faith Farm, but an old rooster with as many lives as the cats who were his friends and companions, could not live forever. When we returned from what was a very rare vacation from our farm, the neighbors who had kindly watched over our four and two-footed family in our absence, shared their concern that Wiley was not eating well. They didn't want to ruin our time away with worries, so they had waited to tell us when we were home once again. Our little rooster seemed too quiet, content to rest in the sun with his eyes closed. We were very worried.

We pleaded with our local veterinarian to take a look at him. Though he was clear with us that birds were outside of his expertise, he agreed to examine Wiley. We wrapped him in a towel and drove quickly to the office. The veterinarian's guess was that he had contracted a virus of some sort. With an impossibly huge needle, he injected an antibiotic into our little bird's breast. Home again, we moved Wiley from the barn to our screen porch and into a box where we could monitor him. Sadly, Wiley was never to return to the barn that had saved him so many years ago. We buried him in what we referred to as our "grotto," a sandy garden area surrounded by ferns just outside our bedroom window so he would be close to us. Wiley was the first and last chicken in our family. Without his crowing each morning the barn was too quiet. It was never the same again.

CHAPTER 4:
Little Cat Feet

"The fog comes in on little cat feet..." Carl Sandburg

For twenty years little cat feet followed the winding drive high above the Cobb River to our farm in southern Minnesota. They followed the dry leaves that autumn winds swirled round in our orchard and deposited on our patio. They carried kittens through wind and soaking rain to our front door. They left tiny ice-encrusted footprints in the snowdrifts that blanketed the fields and surrounded our home and barn.

Weather was usually the catalyst, bringing the little wanderers from their homes and shelters or the dark woods and the green and gold of soybean and corn fields to us. Some were probably deposited by owners at our driveway, assuming their unwanted pet would find a nice farm home. Others may have become lost hunting, or perhaps sought refuge after they were chased by the many predators inhabiting the surrounding fields and woods.

How they found us two-thirds of a mile from the highway, a mile away from the nearest house, twenty minutes' drive from town, we never knew. But magically they came, one after another, year after year seeking a friendly face, food, shelter and safety.

Some of the cats stayed only a little while, enjoying a good meal, a safe place to sleep, a gentle touch before returning to their home or traveling on to another farm, or whatever destiny lay ahead for them.

Some joined our barn cat tribe, occasionally becoming part of our inside cat family. Others found the warm hearts and gentle hands of other people wanting a cat, just like them, to love.

My husband and I moved to our farm with one cat, Tasha. Within a year we added Hallie, a tiny white and orange waif who knew she belonged to us before we suspected it. Four years later, we adopted all six of our neighbor's barn cats who decided in late fall to make the long journey across plowed fields in search of a better life and stayed. We took them all in, not having the heart to send them back, and kept food dishes filled for them, water bowls heated, and heat lights suspended over cushioned beds. Larena, Peaches, Justin, Chess, Jessie and Dancer became permanent residents of our barn and our lives.

Many other cats came to us over the years. We didn't know why they felt they would be safe with us. Perhaps quietening pheromones permeated the air around our farm. Or, as friends and neighbors joked, the cats left a sign directing others to follow the drive to our door. No matter how they came to us, we welcomed them all. Most of them had been owned and loved by someone, somewhere, sometime before us. Only a few were wary of people and shy.

If the cats who came to us stayed for a period of time, we began searching for their owners. We called neighbors, posted pictures and information about them at local stores and veterinary offices, placed ads in local papers and used pet finding internet sites to try to locate their homes. When their owners could not be found, we had them tested for diseases, vaccinated, and neutered or spayed. A large wire-enclosed pen in our barn, built long ago as a chicken coop, became an infirmary and quarantine kennel while we worked to find them a forever home.

A few of the little travelers we brought inside to join our family. We met Kasota, named for his soft yellow fur the color of the limestone bluffs along the river, on a cold winter night walk. We heard him calling above the roar of the river. A veterinarian recommended we bring the tiny tough guy inside to keep him safe following a severe illness. Ghost, a petite cat whose white coat glowed in the moonlight, joined us one Halloween.

Phantom, a huge gray and brown tabby, lived in fear of human contact through most of one winter though we provided him with heated water, food and a warm bed in our shop. The feral tomcat felt all other cats had no right to be on the farm and tried to chase them away. Forced into trapping, neutering and vaccinating him before turning him lose, we expected him to waste no time in leaving our place. But surprisingly he decided to stay and became our gentle giant, provider of prey for the other barn cats, and eventually a sweet cuddly indoor kitty.

Sometimes though, cats found their way to our door but couldn't stay. Sage, a tabby with white and silver-gray fur the color of sage and beautiful emerald eyes, went home one summer day with a fellow member of the Sweet Adeline's chorus I belonged to because he fought with our other cats. A black and white tuxedo only stayed a short time before we took him to the shelter to find his forever home. He had decided the barn loft was his and all other cats were not welcome.

Pictures of the kitties, along with carefully crafted information about them placed in our local paper, quickly brought the right family to find them. We found a handful of bright orange fluff we named Cinnamon crying loudly outside our door one morning.

It was such a long way for a tiny creature to travel to our farm, we suspected that Phantom had carried her to us. He adored her, letting her jump on him and bite his ears, or sometimes dragging her down the barn aisle between his legs. We loved Cinnamon, but she was nearly stomped on by one of my horses when she squeezed under the door to help me clean stalls, so we were tearful but happy when her new family came to take her home.

Sometimes, we made mistakes. April, a little pewter-gray girl with a huge lively personality, had just been placed with her excited new family when my neighbor casually mentioned her gray cat was missing. I had checked with her husband weeks before and he assured me that all their cats were present. I had to tell my neighbor I had placed her cat with another family. I felt badly but I knew April was now in a safer home.

Bright orange Spice had an autoimmune disease that required placement in a single cat household. Through Pet Finders a college student found him and fell in love.

All the cats, whether they lived their entire lives with us or just stayed a short time, enhanced our love and understanding of the amazing creatures. Out of the mist they came to us, on little cat feet, winding around our hearts and intertwining with our lives, if only for a while.

Tasha—Our Silver Girl

I can still feel her in my arms—the soft plushness of her fur, the relaxed weight snuggled against me, her smell. I long some days to have it all be real, but of course it is not. She is gone, but she was a part of my life for so long that the reality of her absence is not as strong as the feeling she is here with me.

Many years before moving to our farm we began our life together, in a less than ideal way, but she eventually found a back door into my heart. Dick and I had just said goodbye to our little Siamese Spiffy after a lengthy illness and finally, hospice care. We weren't looking for another cat, but a co-worker explained that she had rescued a cat from the streets in St. Paul, and she could not keep her. The pound would be her final home unless we adopted her. We decided to take a look. The pewter gray kitten with gold eyes seemed to want no part of us, squirming to get loose from our grasp so she could play with the other cats in the yard. But we couldn't leave her.

We didn't know her breeding, but with the changing gray and

silver patterns of her rabbit-soft fur, we thought maybe Russian Blue. We named her Tasha. Our new kitten was an independent soul. She had personal space requirements which meant holding her was only on her terms. She adored Dick from the beginning, but she treated me with aloofness and sometimes open dislike. I was still grieving the loss of Spiff and not ready to let a new cat into my heart. It was a very rough beginning, but of course the things that we fight hardest against are often just what we need. In fact, I came to need Tasha a great deal.

She was a wildly athletic young cat when she joined our family, jumping high in the air to capture her favorite wire cat-dancer toy over and over again until she was breathless. Our little Burmese Smokey loved her immediately, and she delighted in grooming him, particularly his ears which she washed for hours on end. Tasha was the perfect quintessential mother-cat though she never raised kittens of her own. But there were many other cats who joined our family over the years that she would snuggle and play with and groom. Our silver girl loved them all.

Our young cat had large alert ears that swept in slightly. Bat ears I called them. Her long tail was frequently wound around her front paws. At our first veterinary visit, the doctor told us he believed her to be full grown. But I thought no. With her big paws, it couldn't be. And I was right. She grew into her paws and her tail and became a large girl. The long tail once prevented our losing her. A repairperson working to replace our patio door startled her so badly that she broke through the screen racing out into the yard. It was a quick grab of that long tail that kept her from being a lost soul once again.

Tasha loved food which was evident by her rounded frame. Still, she had delicate movement, walking with her paws placed closely together as if balancing on high heels. She would wind in and around glass decorations on our shelves and walk on the outside of our stair beams while we held our breath waiting for her to fall to the hard tile below.

My father, with his creative imagination, said he thought she was a cross between a cat and another animal. Bear perhaps. But Tasha was all cat. She knew many different words, "birds" being one of her favorites which brought a series of guttural meows rolling from her mouth. Other favorites were "snack" and "outside." Tasha treasured excursions outside on her leash. Not the most cooperative walking companion, she would go along beside us willingly and then fall on her side for a dirt-bath or to investigate a grasshopper. Once down, she was not interested in moving further along despite our urging and gentle tugs on the leash. Ultimately, we'd scoop her up and carry her to another location, and we'd repeat the whole process.

Tasha prowled the expanse of her huge new home with so many rooms on its three floors that finding a way through took mindful thought. She never tired of exploring, having spent almost a year living in the confined spaces of the lake cabin and the apartment. There were many windows ideal for watching birds, squirrels and other wildlife.

She loved us—loved sitting on our laps to watch TV, sleeping with us in bed, waking us with a carefully applied wet nose on closed eyelids. She would sit patiently outside the shower until we emerged and petted her. She did not enjoy being an only cat. She seemed very lonely. We tried to fill the void created by Smokey's death, but people friends are just not as good as cat friends. That is what led us to eventually bring a little barn cat into the house, followed by many other playmates over the years.

When Tasha first began losing weight, we were glad. When we found out the reason, we were dismayed. She had diabetes. The veterinarian assured us, this did not mean the end of Tasha's life. I wondered though if that was true as I attempted for the first time to grab the scruff on her neck and insert the needle that would return her glucose levels to a manageable range.

Twice a day for the rest of her life we administered insulin to help her stay with us. We learned that if Tasha seemed unsteady and disoriented, she was probably suffering from low glucose levels, and we were instructed to quickly administer Karo syrup. In addition to diabetes, she was further diagnosed with amyloidosis. She could not process the food she ingested, and her life was in danger. We had to leave our girl in the hands of a clinic in the Twin Cities. At the clinic, she was fed several times a day with a stomach tube, and we traveled back and forth a hundred miles to visit her at least once each week. It was very hard to leave her behind each time. I worried that she would never eat normally again. But love and dedication can conquer many things.

Once home, we fed her with a syringe through the little tube in her side. She wore baby shirts to keep the tube covered and lessen the danger it might be pulled out accidentally. And she and we survived it all. Giving insulin shots became routine though we had to plan to always be there to give her the required dose within specified times. It wasn't difficult but required careful planning and the help of others to ensure that she received her injections on time.

Through the loss of Smokey, our move to a new town, and a new job, Tasha was there, letting me bury my face in her soft fur, watching patiently with those eyes, softly licking my face. She was so much a part of the family, it seemed she would always be there. On a long-planned family vacation to Lake Tahoe, we received word from the veterinary clinic that Tasha had undergone a low glucose episode. In spite of all efforts, she was in a coma and, though not in pain, would probably not regain full recovery if she survived the episode. We never saw our girl again. Beautiful Lake Tahoe was clouded by our tears and our farm forever seemed too quiet without Tasha's presence.

Hallie—Take Good Care of My Little White Cat

Dick and I settled into Leap of Faith Farm after playing around its edges. Indian summer blessed us with golden days and crisp nights as we began our first year. We'd spent the summer months cleaning out the barn—removing stacks of dusty hay, standing on barrels to reach high overhead to swipe down cobwebs from the rafters, and piling remains of feeding troughs and pans and pails for future disposal. Now, while Dick continued his journey to earn a degree at Mankato State, I began transforming our new house into our home. As I sat on the front steps in late September weather warm enough for shorts, idly pulling weeds from between the bricks and around the remaining flowers, I watched a moving van slowly navigate its bulky cargo around the curve of our road and into our driveway. Soon a sea of boxes, brought out from almost a year-long storage, surrounded me to join the sparse furnishings we had used in our apartment in the past months. Just a few weeks later our attention shifted from unpacking to wedding preparation.

In only two weeks, our home—the quiet retreat we had been seeking for so long—was to be transformed into the site of our wedding and reception. In the whirlwind of settling into our home, we had little time to restore the loveliness of the gardens, orchard, pond and buildings that would help create the setting for our wedding. A week before our big day, Mom and Dad drove from Kansas and worked alongside Dick and me, trimming and removing overgrown shrubs and bringing order to the massive flower beds that had been allowed to grow as they wished for so long. The farm looked much better for all our hard work, but it would be many months, if not years, before it would become truly lovely. Inside, our furnishings looked so at home, people would comment that it looked as though we had been living in our house beside the Cobb River forever.

Tasha for the first time in many months seemed joyous. With three floors to explore in her new home and dozens of rooms, her world had grown greatly from the three rooms we had been living in for the last six months. Sometimes late at night she and I would wander together through the archways and cross the varied tile, wood, and carpeted surfaces, becoming acquainted with this place that felt like a stranger's house, but one we would grow to love.

It was late fall, but a few lingering warm days remained, escorting in our new life on the farm. Early mornings were to be treasured. I couldn't stay away from those first glowing rays that flooded through the east windows of our white Cape Cod home. Tasha roamed those early mornings too, feline dreams awakened by the quiet non-urban sounds. Trees rustled their dry leaves and birds chirped about their busy lives, darting here and there, preparing for the eventual long winter to come.

In the dawning hours, I would slip on Tasha's collar and leash, and we would sit together on the back step overlooking what would become our vegetable garden next spring. Only a giant rhubarb plant and weeds currently grew within its rusty wire enclosure. On other days, we crossed dew-covered grasses pausing at the viewing platform that was constructed beneath a great pine tree at one end of the tiered flower gardens. I hoped I would be fortunate enough to see some of the wildlife that we knew spent quiet nights near our yard. Tasha watched for birds to fly past on their way to and from our feeders.

On one of those bright clear mornings filled with crisp fall air, Tasha and I walked to the little platform overlooking our flowerbed and were surprised to be joined by a tiny cat, barely more than a kitten. She emerged from the pinkish early morning fog, leaped across, and walked carefully along the small water filled ditch that flowed along the garden from the fields, under the pasture run and into our pond. At the point where a trickle of water cascaded over a little rock, the kitten paused for a drink. She was delicate and glowing white in the mysterious light, a fairy cat. Only the swath of orange on her head and a tabby-striped, orange tail convinced me she was real. Tasha felt she was real enough, though, and growled a warning to stay away from her yard and her person.

The kitten seemed only slightly aware that Tasha and I were watching as she repeatedly dipped her paw into the stream and then licked the water away. Finally, no longer thirsty, she lifted her head, turning green eyes at us and continued her journey, blending once more into the fog.

We repeated the ritual for several mornings, separating as we went inside the house to begin our daily routine and the little cat resumed hers. Days later, exploring the farm on a break from wedding preparations, I opened the woodshed door to find a pile of paper feed sacks, discarded on the wood pile and now molded by repeated use, formed into a little nest. "So our visitor has taken up residence," I thought. I worried about her outside in the cold, trying to stay warm on her paper bed. The warm fall would not last.

My sister, brother-in-law, and nephew came from Kansas to help put finishing touches on wedding preparations. My sister and I roamed the fields and edges of the woods, collecting leaves and grasses to augment the floral arrangements from the local florist shop and the dried wreaths that were used to transform the odd non-functioning fireplace on our porch into an altar.

After returning from a trip to the barn loft to enjoy its fabulous view, my sister excitedly told me about the wonderful little white kitten that had joined her on a hay bale by the loft door. She said the kitten was very friendly, extremely affectionate, awfully cute, and seemed to be very much at home in our freshly cleaned upper reaches of the barn. My sister, it seemed, had opened a flood gate of affection from the tiny creature who was also obviously very thin. With the little cat showing no interest in leaving, we gave into feeding her. She hungrily crunched Tasha's dry food and then rewarded us, rubbing on our legs and staring lovingly into our eyes.

The weekend of our wedding day, all my family began arriving. My sister and her family had remained in town, but my mom and dad returned from the ten-hour trip home to Kansas with my uncle and aunt. We were thrilled that everyone was coming to our wedding at our long-dreamed-of farm. My uncle particularly seemed enchanted with the farm. While we worked in the house, discussing plans with the flower shop owner and the caterer, he roamed the outbuildings and fields.

Never having known him to have many pets in his life, we were amazed at the special liking he extended to the little white cat. She apparently had won him over with her purring friendliness. Several times he mentioned what a nice little cat she was.

It rained on our wedding day—slowly drizzling cold mist from heavily overcast clouds, occasionally ushered by gusty winds. A few guests braved the weather to explore our new farm, but most were content to settle inside in the cozy rooms. Tasha was confined to the basement during the comings and goings so she couldn't escape through an open door. Strangely missing was the little white cat, but the rain and cold was a convenient explanation. The wedding on our porch was lovely, and as the rain continued outside, we were warm, gathered with our family and friends.

The next morning, when we went out to say goodbye to my family, there the cat was again, sharing her joy at being among people. My uncle was particularly happy to see her, coaxing her to come close. As they were leaving for the long trip home, he hugged me and said, "Take good care of my little white cat." He explained that he was very worried by her absence the day before, because on returning from a trip with my dad, they had found an unfortunate white cat killed by a car not far from our driveway. They agreed not to tell us before the wedding, thinking it might have been the little cat. Every time I saw my uncle until he died a few years later, he always greeted me with, "How's my little white cat?"

As our lives returned to after-wedding normal, we found a rhythm in the cooling days. And the cat became part of that rhythm. She would appear from nowhere as we worked in the barn or in the overgrown paddocks, insisting we notice her. If we stopped to visit with someone, she joined the conversation. She climbed ladders to be at nose level with the painter. She was the official escort for any visitors. We hadn't wanted a barn cat. We had Tasha and the memory of the little Burmese we had lost only a short time before coming to Leap of Faith Farm. That left a painful place in our lives. But this kitty knew she belonged with us. As the temperature dropped severely, we moved her from her woodshed sacks to a cozy bed in the barn. She became great friends with our Bantam rooster Wiley. Every morning as we opened the barn door, she and Wiley came walking together down the stairs to greet us and the food we provided. Then every night they scaled the steps to the loft once again.

Being responsible pet parents, we took the kitten for her first veterinary visit. She purred so loudly in the warm clinic room that the veterinarian couldn't hear her heart beating. She was vaccinated, treated for worms, and tested for Feline Leukemia Virus which was prevalent in the area. We kept her confined to the chicken coop, in the barn, waiting for the test results. Each day she walked with us on a leash up into the pastures and orchard. We held our breath, exhaling only when the test result was negative. She was a mostly healthy girl.

On Halloween night as the temperature fell below zero for the first time, we made the decision to move her inside, and we named her Hallie for the ghostly night. We couldn't risk exposing Tasha to a few medical issues that accompanied the kitten, so we quarantined Hallie in the basement with a series of stacked folding gates. They could see one another while being kept a safe distance apart.

Hallie plainly loved being inside with us, but cat companionship was not on her agenda. Tasha would come forward offering her kind, sweet friendship, and Hallie would strike at her through the gate mesh. She was a tiny but fearless mite, not strong enough to scale the cat tree we offered as a ladder to the basement windows, but capable of intimidating our large gray cat. All the years we had Hallie, her philosophy on life was to love us unconditionally, but only tolerate other felines.

Poor Tasha. Hallie would ambush and attack her as she did toy mice or bird feather toys. It was many years before she discovered how nice it was to snuggle close to Tasha's large soft body for a nap or to be groomed by her. Hallie's reciprocal grooming started gently, but often those orange ears would quickly flatten against her head, and she would turn licks into chomps accompanied by kicks. She saved the sweet grooming she was capable of for us—licking our faces, our mouths, our eyelids and especially our hair, purring contentedly during the entire session. She found eyelid licks especially helpful in waking us each morning. Over the years, Hallie and Tasha were gradually joined inside our home by Dancer and then Kasota and finally Ghost. But Hallie always felt we were truly hers, on loan to the others.

Hallie played vigorously, looping her tail and skittering across the tile floors in pursuit of real or imagined prey. Unexpected visitors sent her tunneling under the bedspread as soon as they rang the doorbell, but she quickly returned for conversation with them. She climbed into our towel shelves and pulled and pushed them until she created a perfect bed. She burrowed into boxes of Christmas greenery for an impromptu nap. She sat on the bathroom counter watching us brush our teeth and then moved forward to drink water from the faucet. Hallie was intrigued by everything and everyone. She adored our large porch and the birds feeding just beyond the windows, and the frequent walks outside we provided.

In the fall, only a few months after we lost our dear Tasha to diabetes, we found a small lump on Hallie's lower jaw. Feline acne we thought. But the usual remedies did not heal the wound. A biopsy confirmed that she had cancer, but we were assured it was an easily treated form that would not spread or would spread very slowly. We took Hallie to the University of Minnesota Veterinary Medical Center where they removed the tumor. At the same time, we began consulting with a holistic cat veterinarian and began a program to support her fight against the disease. Her diet was restricted to grain-free food and we added supplements, and applied tinctures to strengthen her immune system and maintain her quality of life. Our holistic veterinarian had advised against removing the tumor. She warned of the tiny tendrils that could not be seen that might remain, left behind to grow, and the cancer did grow, returning to cause an ugly sore that eventually interfered with eating and drinking. Our petite cat had to deal with massive growth on her delicate chin. And then we found it had spread.

Hallie's strong personality kept her going, continuing to be our same loving cat in the face of the terrible invader which we learned had moved into her lungs. She had to choose between eating and breathing, and her days became long hours of lying in the protective dark under our bed, pulled reluctantly into the light for medication and feedings and water. She would not give up the fight, but she was becoming weaker. We consulted with an animal communicator to help us gauge Hallie's pain and her thoughts about her illness. She advised us that Hallie would let us know when she no longer wanted to go on. And what Hallie was saying to us was, "Wait."

But one warm spring day, when she continued to hide in the dark, we knew the time had arrived. We heard Hallie's harsh breathing, her moaned acknowledgment of our touch, and with great sadness, called our veterinarian. A short time later, we opened the porch windows to let in the fresh breeze, the bird sounds and the singing wind chimes. We carried her to her favorite room and kissed her goodbye.

I like to believe that somewhere across the rainbow bridge, my uncle was there waiting for her, hearing me say, "Please take good care of my little white cat."

Larena—The Night Visitor

Our first winter at Leap of Faith was a cold and snowy one, a poor time to be learning the intricacies of farm management. We awakened, did chores, and finished our days in the dark, the quietness of the winter night rounding out the day and bringing closure to its challenges. I grew to look forward to the soothing routine of putting on heavy insulating clothes, following the trail through the snow to the barn, and cleaning stalls surrounded by the smell of horses.

Each evening I pushed our wheelbarrow carrying brimming manure buckets to the manure pile. I frequently whistled and sang on my journey while the horses watched with their large brown eyes, hoping I would soon open the barn and invite them into their evening meal of grain and hay and the soft, warm, coziness of their stalls. One very chilly night with snowflakes drifting silently in the halo of barn light, I saw on the path before me a bright orange tabby. She seemed to be waiting there for me. As I moved forward, she mewed and joyfully led the way.

While I dumped the manure buckets, she circled my legs and then rolled on her back in the snow, inviting me to rub her tummy. As I moved off, she sprang to her feet and trotted ahead of me back down the trail. When I opened the barn door, she followed me and sat watching as I led each horse inside, fed them, and secured the stalls for the night.

With the horses safely in their stalls, she approached me once again, intertwining through my legs. When I walked away, back to the house, she stepped back and forth before me, chancing stepped on paws so that I would be sure to notice her. I petted her as we walked along, in that stop and start pattern until I reached the door.

When I disappeared into my warm house, she lingered as if expecting me to ask her in as well. Minutes later when I peered through the window, she was still there, sitting on the step where she had last seen me, paws tucked beneath her, snowflakes covering her orange coat. I wondered how long she would remain and where she would spend the night.

I debated carrying her back into the barn for the night, but shut in our barn, she would have no way to return home. I was sure someone must be looking for her. I reasoned that if in fact she was lost, our woodshed provided good shelter, and if she was still around in the morning, I would try to find her owners. When I hesitantly peeked outside before going to bed, the step was bare. "Goodnight, little cat," I wished her. "I hope you make it safely home."

In the morning, there was no cat, and night chores were completed without her presence. Though I enjoyed her company, I was relieved that she was gone and hoped she was inside and warm. Still, I worried. What if she were a stray, wandering from farm to farm trying to find her people?

Days later, when I thought that she must surely have disappeared, she was there just as before in the pathway to the manure pile. We chatted about where she had gone and why she had returned. With all the chores done, she walked with me to the house and once again lingered on the step when I went inside. Later as I looked out into the moonlight, I saw no feline shadow near our door. She was gone.

Our ritual was repeated several times over the next few weeks. We didn't know where she went in between visits, but she did leave clues. Her home had to be close by. The drifting snow was too deep for her to travel very far. She was also being cared for by someone. Her coat shined and she seemed healthy with a nice layer of fat under it.

Several weeks after the night visits began, neighbors who lived beyond the knoll behind our barn invited us for dinner. Sipping hot chocolate around the table, a flash of orange caught my eye. A moment later my mysterious night visitor strolled calmly into the kitchen and jumped up into a nearby chair.

"This is Larena," our host offered. "We named her after the character in the movie *Lonesome Dove*. She's been our inside cat, but she's been getting into things when we're gone. So, we put her outside. She loves to be in with us and takes every opportunity to sneak back inside. She's really fine outside. She has a good warm place in the barn. But she'd rather be here."

I stroked and scratched her chin as we said goodbyes. "So, you do have a home," I mused, the mystery solved. But it was not to be the end of Larena in our lives at Leap of Faith Farm.

Larena—And Her Family

Larena returned for visits over the winter, spring, and summer. Now that I had met her family, we could chat without my worrying about her when she was out of my sight. It was not until dry corn leaves rustled in the fields and wild geese began their southern flight overhead that our lives became permanently intertwined.

On a chilly late October morning, I hurried to the barn and to the waiting horses. They nickered as I opened the door and called out a greeting. Then, in the crisp air another voice echoed through the barn, the loud cry of a cat in distress. Climbing quietly up the stairs, I peered into the darkened loft. Expecting to find a full-grown cat there, I was amazed when a tiny kitten only several inches tall toddled toward me.

"Where did you come from?" I asked the yellow fur ball. As I reached to pick up the bundle, the terrified kitten hissed and disappeared into the safety of the hay bales. "I'll be back later, kitten," I promised and hurried down to feed my impatiently pacing horses.

After my husband and I finished chores, we again traveled up into the loft. This time, I moved more quietly, and I was gradually able to reach out to touch the tiny creature. "Shall we feed it something?" I asked Dick. He rolled his eyes in reply. The pattern was a familiar one of feeding kittens and cats for just a few days that extended into a permanent arrangement. But neither of us could deny the tiny mews that now came from our loft resident. We brought cat food from the house and sat back watching as the kitten eagerly devoured our offerings. We decided to leave the door open that day, confident that the mother cat must be nearby and would return to claim her baby. The little kitten could not have climbed steps twice its height or navigated the half mile or so that separated our farm from our neighbors without assistance.

I hurried to the barn that evening, eager to see that our prediction was correct, and that mother cat and babe had been reunited. My sureness changed to astonishment when I reached the loft to find not an empty room, or even a little kitten and its mother, but four more cats of assorted sizes and colors! As I stood at the top of the stairs allowing my eyes to adjust to the dim light, six pairs of eyes peered out at me from the surrounding hay bales. The cats watched, ready to spring. And then, one of them strolled forward, the kitten bounding at her side, and wound herself around my legs, purring happiness. Larena had returned for another visit and had brought her family.

My husband called out from below, "Is the kitten gone?" "Not exactly," I replied. "You better come up and see." His reaction was like mine. Total disbelief. Larena had managed to not only carry the tiny little kitten to our farm across rough plowed fields and woods, but to encourage the other cats to come with her. We could only guess what had motivated them to leave their home and journey across frozen fields to our barn, but we were touched by the trust the cats had in Larena, and by her trust in us. We were caught between the practicality of caring for six semi-feral cats, and the honor Larena had given us of caring for her family. Our neighbors, when we called, thanked us for letting them know where their cats had gone, and offered to bring them home. But when they arrived with kennels the following night, the cats refused to be caught, darting in and out of hay bales. We agreed to gradually bring the cats back as we were able to capture them. And over time we would determine their future.

Outside the snow began to fall, giant flakes swirling in the wind. Winter is a time for settling down in the northern Midwest. It isn't a time for changing homes or being out in the night. I worried immediately about the cats that had come to us and what would become of them. In our barn, I knew they would be cared for as long as they wished to stay.

"It will all work out," Dick said, as he says in many situations where I invest hours of debate and rationalizing. If the cats were going to be our guests for a while, we decided to make them comfortable in our cold loft. We bought and hung heat lamps over cozy nests made from blankets within a circle of hay bales. We put out fresh water and installed cat pans to tempt them away from piles of hay on the floor. Best of all, to their liking, we purchased a good supply of kitten and cat food and made sure the bowls were filled each morning and night.

Over the next few days, we were able to pet and gradually pick up the little yellow kitten whom we had first found in the loft. He loved to play, chasing strings and straw in the sunlight that streamed through the loft window. He jumped and played with such agility and grace that I named him "Sundance" and "Dancer" for short.

"Don't name them," my husband cautioned. But the names just kept coming. An orange and white adult female, I named "Peaches" for her peaches and cream coloring as well as her slightly ditsy personality. A very regal three quarters grown buff colored male became "Justin." The sweet black and white kitten would be "Chess" and the tiny gray kitten with a lightning bolt on her chest I called "Jessie" because she told me that was her name.

We believe strongly that controlling pet population is a responsibility of pet ownership. The ghosts of those poor little kittens that didn't survive long enough to travel to our barn haunted us. And so, we approached our neighbors with an offer. We would make appointments and pay half the cost of vaccinating, neutering, and spaying the cats if they would pay the other portion. They eagerly agreed. The plan was that I would somehow trap the cats and then, when they were well, return them to our neighbors.

Over the next few weeks, we methodically encouraged the cats to come in the kennel for their morning and evening feedings, always leaving the door open for their escape. We were finally successful in capturing the three kittens in one kennel. Larena and Peaches were trapped a short time later. It seemed harsh treatment for the kittens that we were trying otherwise to care for gently with quiet movement and soft words, but kittens having more kittens would only compound problems for the cats and for us.

Everyone survived the ordeal. I called our neighbors reporting on the success of our efforts, and we talked again about returning the cats. But when I drove my cargo back from the veterinarian, my Jeep wanted to turn into my drive rather than continue down the road, and I did not object. We'll just wait till spring, we decided. But that particular spring at Leap of Faith Farm never happened. Larena and her family continued to live happily in our loft. We worked very hard to tame the semi-feral felines and could gradually pet and briefly pick up all of them. They each grew to tolerate yearly visits to the veterinarian for vaccinations and routine treatments for injuries and illness.

You never know when you make a friend, where that relationship will lead you. Through her intelligence and friendship with her neighbors, Larena found a way to assure the future of her family. We experienced the joy of learning more about our farm and ourselves through the unique personalities of six wonderful cats.

Dancer—On a Sunbeam

Not long after we decided to make all the cats our own, Dancer did not scamper down the stairs to greet me one morning. He sat in his favorite sunbeam patch, coughing and sneezing. When I called, he looked at me with half-closed eyes. His nostrils were filled with mucus, and matter crusted in the corners of his eyes. He was a very sick kitten, and I feared that unless we acted quickly, Dancer might not be part of our family for long. I called our veterinarian who suggested we try to feed him some warm broth with an eye dropper, clean his eyes and nose, and see how he was the next morning. He loved the broth, but he was no better the next day.

As soon as the veterinary office opened, I held our tiny charge in the palm of one hand, tight against me, as Dick drove. He was diagnosed with an upper respiratory herpes virus. Probably the other cats who were coughing and sneezing also had the virus but were too unapproachable to treat.

Dancer snuggled against my shoulder seeming to enjoy our conversation as I gently stroked his tiny head with my finger. We were worried about the baby and talked about the possibility of bringing him inside to join our other cats, assuring each other that he was fine in the barn. "But he is so tiny," my mind argued, "and we saved his life." Oblivious to the planning of his future, Dancer slept within the bed of my hands.

Our veterinarian cautioned that Dancer was a very sick kitten and might not survive, but we immediately began treating him and Larena with antibiotics. He loved the pink bubblegum-scented medicine, eagerly coming to receive an eyedropper full each morning and night. Over the next few days, he gradually became a scampering elf once again. Intent on capturing the baling twine I dangled before him, he leaped through patches of sunlight streaming through the loft windows.

He seemed better, but when the cough and sneezes persisted in spite of medication, the veterinarian recommended moving him into a warmer place until his symptoms completely disappeared. One evening after feeding, we carried the kitten up the stairs into the finished attic over our garage. It was cozy and would keep him safe. Sadly, it also would keep Dancer apart from his family and isolated from our inside cats who might contract the disease. It was the first big step into becoming an inside cat and finding his way deeper into our hearts. I grieved with Larena for her loss, but I knew that separation was important for the well-being of both baby and mother.

"It's too bad there isn't another kitten you can put with him," the veterinarian told us. But the only choices for companionship were his almost wild cousins who were also infected. Little Dancer had to learn to be by himself away from his mother and the family he loved. The kitten spent much of his days alone with the sound of a radio for company and visits and play sessions as often as we could manage them. It was not a good life for a baby kitten.

He was lonely and delighted in our human company, racing to greet us when he heard our footsteps on the stairs. We lay on the floor, cuddling his wiggly soft body. He nestled against my husband's chest as he read, contentedly pulling on Dick's shirt buttons with his little mouth. He learned to be an expert retriever hurtling over our outstretched legs and returning stuffed mice or wadded up paper balls for another toss. He jumped several feet in the air catching toys and bringing them to us. He was cozy in his attic tower, but we hated confining him there, and worried about the long-term impact his isolation would cause.

One night as snow swirled outside and loss of power caused our lights to flicker and then grow dark, we ended Dancer's confinement. Without electric heat in the loft, he would be very cold. Up the garage stairs I went, returning with a chilled Dancer and settling him on my lap by our wood-burning stove. He never left the warmth of our home and family. Motherly Tasha claimed him immediately. Straddling him she held him down for a good grooming session. Hallie tolerated him but never interacted with him beyond a good chase game. Kasota, who came to join our inside cat family later became his friend.

Over the years, his light orange coat changed to a bright red and white. True to belief that red cats are high strung, Dancer was a very smart and sensitive guy. He was insecure in new surroundings and would hiss at anything unfamiliar. While the other cats loved going outside on leashes for walks, he would cry and reach up with his paws, begging to be picked up and carried. He often saw the barn cats, his mom and the rest of his family, but he only watched them, seeming to have no interest in getting closer.

We always felt very badly about keeping Dancer apart from his family for so long. But his love for us and sweetness never wavered. He would nestle inside my arms for as long as I allowed him to stay, and at night he would curve his body across the top of my head and sing me to sleep with his purring. He brought me countless sparkle balls, played catch endlessly, and pounced and skidded across our floors in pursuit of red laser toy beams.

His deep green eyes forever looked trustingly into mine. An amazing boy who survived the odds against survival—our bright red kitten, our Sundancer.

Jessie—Sweet Spirit Lit by a Lightning Flash

Of the kittens that joined Leap of Faith Farm that winter, Jessie seemed the most friendly. Just a tiny waif of a cat, she was a sweet girl with a wild, strong spirit. She had green eyes and a cream calico coat with such subtle markings she appeared to be a solid soft gray. A gold lightning bolt flashed across her chest and cream patches decorated her paws. A baby of mixed heritage, she had a round face and flat nose of a Persian with hooded eyes like Larena, a rail thin body and a long tail that hooked at the tip when she was happy.

Jessie was a smart girl. Quickly associating us with food, she tolerated mealtime petting long before the other cats. She loved being near and watching us. She chirped cheerful greetings when we approached and always trotted before us back and forth to the barn. Winding in and out between our legs, she would stop just out of our reach, a coquette inviting pets and shoulder scratches before scampering away evading us.

Believing that Jessie's trust in us had grown to the point where she could be handled safely, I decided to pick her up one morning as she ate her breakfast. With amazing speed our girl began to struggle, twisting and turning in my grasp and strangely trapping a front tooth under my ring. I wanted to set her free as desperately as she wanted to flee, but for a few moments we were stuck there, she and I. Unfortunately, because she felt scared and trapped, she bit down on my poor finger. I was finally able to drop her not so gently onto the floor. I felt terrible that my poor judgement had frightened our little cat and damaged the trust she had slowly built in her human caretakers. After years of patiently petting and coaxing, we were eventually able to pick her up again and cuddle her briefly before she began struggling to return to the ground. Still, we could never fully rebuild the relationship we had with Jessie and the trust she had in us.

When strangers came to the farm, Jessie bravely ventured down the stairs from the loft to watch them, making sure they never got too close. As winter approached each year and we started piling on our winter clothes for chore-time in the barn, she hid from us. I don't think she quite believed that her people were really under all those coats and heavy winter boots. In the spring when we shed those heavy layers, our warm sweet Jessie emerged again.

She was a terror during veterinary visits. On her first trip after a deceptively quiet car ride, I watched helplessly as she thrashed violently on the exam table. Squirming out of the veterinarian's grasp, Jessie fell to the floor. Realizing her newfound freedom, she raced forward around the room knocking over bottles and equipment until the veterinarian and I were able to trap her beneath a blanket on the floor. We kept her under cover of the blanket, carefully pulling out a little leg for injections. On our second visit, another veterinarian and his assistant held Jessie down for an exam and vaccines before returning her thankfully to her carrier. Anticipating the worst on our third visit, we cautiously explained to yet another veterinarian that she had been difficult to handle in the past. In astonishment we watched as the doctor easily tipped her out of her carrier, examined the perfect little lady who sat posing quietly on the table, vaccinated her, and sent us on our way. From then on, he was Jessie's doctor.

Jessie was generally very healthy, having only one serious problem that required confinement in our chicken coop infirmary. We noticed her limping. At first, we thought she had injured a paw or a leg racing through the barn or playing with the other cats. We were relieved when the problem seemed to disappear. But then she began limping again, and we decided to have her examined. The doctors found a surprising cause. One of her claws had grown very long and had curved back into her foot pad. A nail trim and some antibiotics, and Jessie was her playful self once again. During her treatment and confinement in the chicken coop in our barn, Jessie grew more tame, easy to pick up and medicate. But she was sad in her confinement and depression interfered with her eating. We finally set her free to be with the others.

Jessie loved playing by herself or with Chess who sometimes stalked and attacked her. She scampered after dry leaves in the barn aisle and adored a strangely misshapen blue plastic ball. She chased the flat-sided ball in and out of stalls, always leaving it somewhere my big warmblood horse Lars would notice it. Every time he spied her toy he would flash his ears forward, bring his nose to the ground to sniff the foreign thing, and then move in a wide circle around the frightening object. Perhaps Jessie left it there for the fun of watching his reaction.

She loved her mom, Larena, who generally would hiss or growl at her signs of affection. Jessie ignored her responses and continued to rub her nose or run her face along Larena's side. In spite of Larena's objections, Jessie continued to try to cuddle tightly against her reluctant companion, finally winning her over. They would often roam the orchard or hayfield together, almost as if she knew how vulnerable she was; Jessie rarely strayed far from the farm. Even though Larena seemed to barely tolerate Jessie's friendliness, she was a strong defender of her baby when she perceived a threat was near. She would position herself between Jessie and the occasional stray, growling warnings and even chasing the intruder away from her little one.

Only ten years after coming to us, Jessie sat looking at me through the wire mesh of the carrier as we drove to the clinic. She studied my face, not with fear in her eyes, but interest as if wondering what I was thinking about her. I was lost in disbelief. How could those coughing and sneezing episodes, symptoms of a herpes virus she had since coming to our barn, turn into a violent invasion of her tiny body? An abscessed tooth we thought, not good, but treatable. Still, the discharge from her nostril and the watering, mattered eye that had recently appeared, scared us. These things together made our veterinarian suspicious. In just days, laboratory results confirmed squamous cell carcinoma—a fast-advancing form of cancer.

Jessie's tiny muzzle swelled and then began bleeding. Within days she stopped eating. We lavished her with attention, and she seemed to love the petting, brushing and loving words we fed her instead of food. We made the decision not to sustain her with a feeding tube, our little wild cat who was so fearful of people and strange places. The prognosis was not good, no matter what treatment could be offered, although we researched all options with two university hospitals.

Jessie lived in the chicken coop in the barn, with a heat light and heated cushion disks under her blankets keeping her warm, as the cold pre-Christmas winds blew snow against the window. She cried to be with the other cats, but we wanted to be able to reach her to provide the little help we could—pain relief medication we applied on her ears. Jessie remained cooperative, accepting our help quietly. Her breathing grew more labored each day, and still she remained the tough little cat she had always been, sharpening her claws on the worn post inside the coop as she and the other cats had done ever since the barn became their home.

We boarded her at the clinic while we traveled home to Kansas for Christmas for a few days. The reports were never good when we checked about her condition. They said she was difficult to treat and was not doing well. We brought her home as soon as we returned and placed her back in the security of the coop, but when she cried, alone in her little bed, we relented and released her. With a strength unsupported by any nourishment, she climbed the stairs to the loft to be reunited with her family. Phantom, Larena and Chess, after carefully sniffing her strange hospital smells, welcomed her into their warm little nest beneath the lights and within the circle of hay bales in the loft.

This kitten, who should have died as a baby because she was so frail, so difficult to help, so difficult to love, survived and lived a good life at Leap of Faith Farm. She was an incredibly tough, brave girl and, as the technician at the hospital said when we at last took her there, she fought hard for a long time. Jess continued to be herself, to live the life of a cat, even though everything within her was changing—until the end.

I can still see Jessie, stretched out on the wicker rocker on our patio, absorbing the warm sun. I see her sitting in the barn doorway with her long tail wrapped carefully around her. I look for her trotting in front of us, hooked tail waving in the air, escorting us along the drive or walking with us and the other cats up into the orchard to pick bright red apples on a crisp fall afternoon.

Peaches—A Face at the Window

I never made the morning trip from our house to the barn without glancing up at the loft window, expecting to see Peaches watching for me. We had placed a hay bale there just for her—a window seat to the world where she could watch us and the coming and goings of our farm from a safe distance. Peaches has been gone for five years now, but I still look for her. It's an unrealistic exercise, I know, but because we never found any trace of her after that last Labor Day weekend when she came racing from the soybean field calling to us, a part of me has never been sure she is not out there somewhere.

A probable kitten of Larena, she came to us full grown. The relationships between Larena and Peaches and the multiple kittens of varying ages that accompanied them to our farm were never clear. Perhaps she was mother to a litter of babies that did not survive, or to the fortunate Dancer who was carried by one of them across the fields to find a home in our barn. Peaches and Larena shared mothering duties to the tiny to almost-grown babies, and treated them all with devoted attention. While Larena ruled the tribe, Peaches loved them all.

Peaches is the reason that we adopted our neighbors' cats, all five of them at one time. When they traveled across the barren field between our farms thirteen years before and found shelter and food in our hay loft, it was that little orange and white cat that changed "their cats"to"our cats." When our neighbors came with a kennel to take their cats home, Peaches was the first cat they attempted to lift into the kennel. But she had other ideas about leaving her new home, leaping out of my neighbor's arms and fleeing down the barn aisle. And so, we agreed to try again another time. We kept the kennel on loan, but it never made a laden trip back to the neighbors' farm. We returned it months later after all the cats had been lured into it, captured, and taken to the veterinary clinic for spaying, neutering and vaccinations.

The sweet but skittish white and orange girl never became completely tame. Though we could pet her on occasion, she remained wary. She allowed herself the luxury of hands stroking her fur when she ate her meals, but she had an uncanny ability to always detect any small change in our behavior that would indicate we wanted to do more than give her a brief pet. She would duck through our outstretched hands seconds before we could close them around her to pick her up.

And yet she was surprisingly cooperative when we finally subdued her. For there were times, when she was ill or when we needed to take her to the clinic for yearly veterinary examinations and vaccinations, that she acted much like any house cat. The return to the barn, however, proved her briefly passive nature was not her true self. For days afterwards, we could not coax her into the chicken coop where the cats were fed, and only when we moved away some distance down the barn aisle, did she venture inside. Even then, any movement toward her sent her scurrying.

I named her Peaches, partly because of her peaches and cream coloring, but also because of her consistently sweet personality. She would run to greet us when we walked from the house to the barn to do chores, circling us and winding in and around our legs. Maddeningly, she would sometimes abruptly stop, leaving us mid-stride with the option of tripping over her or stepping on her little white paws. Often she would sit before us on her haunches, reach up and grab Dick's or my hand in her front paws, and lick it to show her affection. Her purr was loud and strong and could be heard some distance away.

Peaches was the one cat in our barn tribe that Larena seemed to like. They slept together frequently and shared the same food bowls. Unlike her mom, Peaches was sweet-tempered and loved all the other cats. She also loved to climb. A favorite perch was a small catalpa tree that grew beside a section of fence just outside the old woodshed. She and the other cats would race up the tree or sit on the two fence posts surveying our comings and goings.

On one visit to our veterinarian, they discovered a broken tooth. We were never sure how it had happened, perhaps from a fight with another cat, but the tooth had to be removed. After surgery, Peaches was confined for a week in the chicken coop while we battled with her, trying to treat possible infections with antibiotics. Our sweet girl did not like to be constrained or medicated. She twisted and turned like a little snake, shutting her eyes and her mouth tightly against any medication we tried to apply or inject.

We worried about Peaches over the years because she seemed to have a wanderlust to her spirit. All of our cats were hunters and roamed freely around our property and beyond. Peaches often left on field trips, a companion to Larena or Justin, exploring and hunting all day and returning home for dinner and a cozy bed at night. Peaches, unfortunately, took her hunting trips seriously, sometimes being gone for several days at a time. Just as we had almost given up on seeing her again, there she would be, trotting down the drive escorted by the other cats, and then joining them in the barn for breakfast or dinner.

Late one summer, we noticed a change in our girl. She wasn't eating well and seemed to prefer spending the late summer days lying near our patio among yellow mums against the warmth of our house foundation. She came down from the barn loft each day to be with the other cats, but she didn't seem herself, not really sick but just different. We watched for any other changes that indicated we needed to intervene with more care but saw nothing to alarm us.

Labor Day weekend gave us extra time for doing fall chores and opportunities to play including the chance for a late afternoon ride. We came home just as the sun was starting to set, put the horses away and went up to the house. Just before we entered the garage, we heard loud meowing coming from the field—the same sounds over and over. We turned and saw Peaches racing towards us as fast as she could run. When we stopped to pet her, she purred and rubbed against our legs, obviously thrilled to be with us. Something seemed to have upset her, and I felt she was trying to tell us about it, but as I surveyed the field and looked toward the barn where the other cats were settling in for the night, nothing seemed out of place. We thought maybe we should walk her down to the barn but we were hungry and tired, and she was used to traveling the short distance almost every day, so we said, "Goodnight," and went inside to our human activities, leaving her behind.

When we went to feed the animals in the morning, Peaches was not among them. We hoped that this would be like her other overnight adventures, and she would magically reappear ready to travel with us to the barn, but the evening before was to be the last time we would ever see her. We called neighbors, put ads in all the papers, posted her picture at veterinary offices, checked with the pound and put notices up at stores in the community. We followed every lead, every call from someone who had seen an orange and white cat, but not our orange and white girl. Gradually we grew to accept that Peaches was gone. I asked farmers to watch for signs of her when they worked their fields, but no one ever found any evidence of what happened to her. It was as though she had vanished.

Months later an animal communicator told us that Peaches had been trying to tell us for some time she was hurting. Her meows were her last attempt to gain our attention and our understanding that she had a pain in her stomach and she was trying to help herself heal. The communicator felt Peaches was somewhere nearby, but we never found her. And so I still watch for her, as I'm sure she is watching for us, and remember the haunting meows from that last time together.

Justin—A Golden Cat with Green Eyes

I knew his name the minute I saw him. Justin. Quietly regal, his name suited the large soft gold kitten with emerald eyes. He was a buff-colored tabby, long and lanky, with a narrow softly marked face ending in the surprise of a pink nose, a tractable giant who was always the most approachable of all the barn cats. He was wise, observant, kind to us and a wonderful older brother to the rest of the tribe as well as a calm confident leader next in line to Larena.

He welcomed our attention and was tolerant of occasional routine medical attention, only making soft cries when his foot was accidentally closed in the kennel door in a frenzied effort to secure him for an annual trip to the veterinarian. Justin welcomed the life we provided him and seemed appreciative, knowing what life could be outside our cozy loft. He only became worried when he thought he was excluded from the warm world of the barn and its safe hay loft. A memory remains of looking out our window toward the barn and seeing Justin's back legs and long gold tail as he scrambled frantically to squeeze through a four-inch opening at the bottom of our big barn door when he had mistakenly been left outside.

Of all the cats, Justin's favorite companion was Kasota, a smaller version of Justin who came to the farm one cold winter night several years after Justin's family arrived. Kasota was a reflection of Justin with his golden coat and those same knowing green eyes. But where Justin was rangy and long, Kasota was compact and rounded. The two golden cats were almost inseparable buddies. Mutt and Jeff, they roamed the farm together walking side by side, their yellow striped tails intertwining.

Justin loved us and he loved his life at Leap of Faith Farm which he patrolled continually to make sure all was well. Like Larena, there was something within him though that caused him to sometimes wander far away, frequently traveling with Kasota or Larena and Peaches. Often he would walk with us as we did chores or strolled through our hayfield or orchard. But sometimes Justin made solitary journeys to a place, that for reasons only he knew, drew him from us. We knew when he was planning to leave because he would begin saying goodbye to everyone. He would visit with Larena and each of his siblings—touching noses and rubbing faces, and then we would see him go—walking stealthily across the orchard or hay field into the woods, drawn by something that called to a place deep inside him. He would sometimes be gone only a day or two, or sometimes we would not see our green-eyed boy for two weeks or more. Then, he'd appear once again, strolling into the yard or orchard, as if he'd only been returning from a visit to his favorite observation haunt beneath the bird feeders behind our house.

His reappearance was always met with great jubilation by his family. They would rub their faces against him and intertwine tails as they walked with him back to the barn murmuring, "Welcome home." Within a short time, everyone would settle back into their routines, and it would be as though he had never gone.

It was fall, harvest time, and all the cats were in the orchard with us as we picked shining red apples from our trees. Justin joined in, then he began his ritual—talking to each of the cats. We watched him as he quietly slipped away into the surrounding woods.

Weather was turning cold, and we began calling neighbors when we had seen no sign of him for several days. It was not like Justin to be away from his warm bed with the coming of chilly nights. No one had seen our golden boy. Late October arrived, and Dick and I had for some time planned a trip to Kansas for my father's birthday. We were driving home when I started talking again about Justin and my worry that we would never see him again. It was then that Dick casually mentioned he had seen my darling guy.

My husband had been on an evening walk just before our trip when he saw Justin walking toward him along our long gravel drive. Justin approached him and wanted to be petted. When Dick turned for home, Justin started to follow him, but then, hearing a noise nearby in the woods, bolted away. Dick called to him, thinking that Justin would realize how close he was to his home, and then find his way to the barn which was always left open in the hope that he would return.

My husband assumed that Justin would gradually make that last little bit of his journey down our road, but he never did. For a very long time, driving home down the highway to our farm, I would slow down hoping my eyes would not find a poor cat lying beside the road. I searched whenever I rode the horses out across the fields or down by the river that bends around our land. The orchard is haunted by the last memory I have of him slipping into the shadows of the woods. I miss his quiet, wise green eyes watching me. Justin, lost forever.

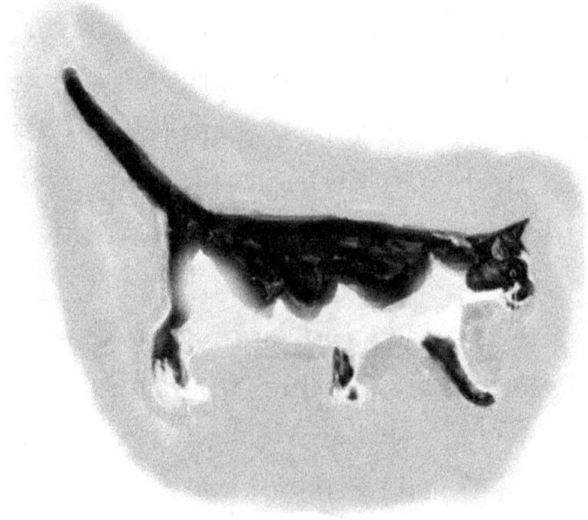

Chess—The Cat with Twelve Lives

I finally put away the medicines, the supplements, the tinctures that had supported Chess over the last two and one-half years—two years beyond the most positive prognosis for his survival.

We were away for the weekend searching for a home for him, our other four cats and two horses in Kansas when we got the call from our animal sitter that Chess didn't look right. A video confirmed that he was having seizures, and I urged her to take him to our veterinarian right away. Our veterinarian kept him under constant surveillance day and night, but he continued to deteriorate. Chess had so many things wrong with him, too many for the gentle black-and-white cat with the dark green eyes to withstand any longer.

Chess stood out from all the other cats at our farm, his black-and-white coat a departure from the yellows and whites, and even the grays of his family. He was one of the older kittens to travel across the field to our farm with the rest of his family, and to make the barn at Leap of Faith Farm his home.

Chess was very sweet and very shy. He loved chasing strings as well as the end of my whip dragged across the ground, but he was easily frightened and never approached us except at feeding time. Chess turned to Jessie and Justin for companionship. We were clearly not part of his social world. We worried how we would ever persuade him to let us get near and hoped a reason to test his reluctance was a long time away.

When he was several years old, we noticed that he was scratching his right ear and holding it at an odd angle. We captured the elusive patient and transported him to our veterinary clinic where they found a polyp deep inside the ear canal. They were reluctant to remove it and referred us instead to the University of Minnesota Veterinary Center in St. Paul. He and I were roommates at the motel overnight while we waited for his early morning appointment. Chess, who had never lived inside any structure except the barn, spent the night under the bed with brief excursions for food, water and kitty pan, while I slept above him. The next day the hospital removed the growth which thankfully was benign, and we returned to the farm. It was to be the first of many trips to the university with Chess.

Chess had several behaviors that further distinguished him from the other cats in his family and that we found endearing. We fed our barn cats no-grain food and bottled water after treating several urinary infections over the years. Chess came to eat with all the other barn cats, but he had a unique feeding habit. He would scoop each crunchy out with a paw and then gobble it down, or alternatively, extend his upper jaw over the rim of the bowl and pull food into his mouth with his lower jaw. He often used his paw creatively in drinking water as well. He would dip his paw into the water bowl and then lick water from it.

Chess enjoyed being outside playing and luxuriating in dust baths, his white fur often a dingy gray from rolling on our gravel driveway and in the barn aisle. It was when his mid-length coat took on a greasy appearance. and his weight began dropping no matter how much he ate, that we became concerned. Blood tests revealed that, just like Tasha, Chess was diabetic. It is one thing to manage diabetes in an inside cat who loves affection and is used to being handled; it is another to manage diabetes in an outdoor cat who is fearful of people and whose favorite pastime is hunting and eating wild prey. But we tried.

We began with a topical treatment rubbing medication inside his ears as he ate his meals with the other cats, but his glucose levels continued to be dangerously high. We sometimes used our chicken coop as a kennel to treat minor injuries in the barn cats or to house stray kitties who wandered along the Cobb River down the driveway to our farm, so we turned to it to treat Chess. When we were successful in confining him, he became a purring machine, easy to treat and never aggressive. But the moment the coop door opened, Chess was gone. The next step became clear when, after consuming the trophy from his latest hunt one day, his glucose levels took a life-threatening turn. We sped along the two-hour trip to St. Paul where doctors worked desperately to save him. After several days, he did get better again, but another illness had surfaced—pancreatitis. The diagnosis brought a huge change in Chess's and our lives.

It was clear that Chess could no longer be maintained outside. He needed regularly scheduled insulin injections, and he was placed on an exotic protein diet. He could eat nothing related to foods that his body was familiar with, so common cat foods were not permitted. We began feeding him a diet of wild caught salmon and venison. After adding homeopathic supplements prescribed by the holistic veterinarian we consulted with, Chess's digestive system came under control and he began gaining weight.

When the weather became too cold for his weakened condition to be managed through the food we were providing, we put Chess in a carrier and toted him up into the loft above the garage. The loft—a furnished apartment with lights, carpeting, heat and air conditioning that had provided temporary housing for staff at nearby Minnesota State University—had been home to Dancer three years earlier. Chess, whose paws had only experienced wood planks, concrete, and hay bales felt the carpet beneath his feet, felt the warm heat surrounding him, and purred his contentment and gratitude. But just like Dancer, the comfortable home we moved him to came with a price. He was isolated from what remained of his barn cat family. It would be a lonely life for poor Chess. We tried to compensate by spending more time with our little cat, going upstairs throughout the day to feed him and monitor his condition, and to give him insulin injections and the other medications he needed.

Chess was a fighter but another adversary confronted him. Having survived his other illnesses, we felt his luck had run out when he was diagnosed with multiple myeloma with lesions appearing on his liver and spleen. University of Minnesota doctors told us sadly that radiation and chemotherapy were his only hope, and then he would not survive more than one and a half years. Without the treatments, he would live only three months. Chess had come so far, and now we were being told his treatment would require that he stay for long periods of time away from us, and the cost was a tremendous amount given the outcome.

As we were pondering the options, one more condition was placed on our little cat's body. He had cardiomyopathy. Because of his heart disease, chemotherapy to treat Chess's cancer had been taken off the table. The decision, though, opened a window to a much gentler approach to help him. Working with our holistic veterinarian in consultation with our local veterinarian we devised a treatment plan, blending traditional western medicine with eastern medicine to keep him comfortably with us as long as possible. And it worked for a long time.

Life became better for Chess when, because of increasing summertime heat levels in the loft, we moved him downstairs into our utility and mud room. My inside cats were not happy about this change. They liked to lounge on the cat tree in the utility room, lie on clean baskets of clothes, and watch us from their window perch as we worked outside in the garden, and Chess's residency prevented them from doing these things. Eventually we began letting him out to mingle with them. They grew to accept Chess in their midst but never welcomed him. Ghost, our young female, delighted in ambushing him and gleefully watched as he retreated back into his quarters.

Chess became a different cat through all the medical adventures and treatment. I believe he knew we had saved his life. He was a sweet, affectionate loving cat, stretching on his side and pawing the air when his belly was rubbed and his chin was scratched. He showed his affection for us with head butts, and we frequently put our faces close to his so he could bump our foreheads. He learned to enjoy the outdoors he had roamed vicariously, watching birds and squirrels from windows or porch benches. Perhaps one of his low glucose events had resulted in some neurological change, for he never seemed as active as he had once been, and sometimes seemed confused. And yet he loved to play, chasing and jumping at twirling bird toys and red laser rays.

He sat and watched the other cats cuddling with us on the couch or napping on a throw, but only rarely would he become brave enough to jump up beside us. But once there, his purrs reverberated through the room. After moving Chess inside the house, and with his illnesses more effectively managed, I started brushing him regularly, pulling handfuls of gray fuzzy undercoat free and leaving his white-and-black coat shiny and silky. He learned to walk on a leash outside with us. We walked around the yard and down to his much-loved barn. I think he must have wondered where all his friends were, now that no meows of greeting came from the dark open door. But he seemed pleased to be there.

Chess was doing well after a change in his diet to address an intolerance he had developed for his long-time venison diet. His ears were upright and alert, and his eyes were bright. He was more social once again, and the other cats had begun to groom him. "He's a miracle cat," our veterinarian said. "He just keeps going in spite of all his illnesses—instead of nine lives, he has twelve." We laughed and said goodbye, not knowing our next conversation would be about the end of his life.

We rushed through chores that last morning with Chess, eager to be on our eight-hour drive to visit my family in Kansas. He seemed a little shaky when he followed me to get his food dish, but he ate well, liking the new food and licking it from my fingers. Yet as I was giving him his injection, just for a moment, those green eyes caught my attention. He looked into my soul, and I thought, "Chess, are you telling me goodbye?" He wandered through the house with the other cats, and they all watched us pack the dreaded suitcases that meant we would be leaving them soon.

We hesitated before loading the Jeep and discussed whether we should take the time to bring him into town for a final check, just to be sure he was all right before we left. But, we convinced each other that he was fine, and our caretaker would call if there were problems. She did, in fact call that evening to say Chess was acting strangely. I called the clinic and arranged for our veterinarian to stay at her clinic until our caretaker came in with Chess. Our little boy was having seizures, and over the next few days, in spite of our dear veterinarian's round-the-clock care, we agreed that he was slipping from us.

Days later I retrieved the empty pink kennel and Chess's ashes within a box wrapped in velvet cloth. The kennel rattled an empty reminder all the way to the farm. Through teary eyes, I whispered, "I promised I would bring you home, Chess." For our little black-and-white Chess, his last life had run out.

Phantom—The Feral Cat with a Heart of Gold

We saw him all that summer, slinking between flower beds and bushes, watching us as we went about our farm life. There one minute, and gone the next, a phantom cat vanishing into the peony bushes, slipping between the tall stalks of Queen of the Prairie, or peeking from beneath cool hosta foliage. When we approached him, he hurried away in his long bow-legged stride into the cornfields or nearby woods.

It was during a visit from my parents that we first began to really notice him. My dad asked about the black cat sitting on our utility room steps. Just another stray, we thought. A drifter, following whatever signs there are around Leap of Faith Farm that directs cats to our doorstep and a welcoming reception. We saw the cat on our steps, but he was not black. Instead, we found a strikingly handsome gray and black tiger-striped tabby. When we caught a brief glimpse of his eyes, they were yellow-green and huge. Yet, as we watched his retreat, the tabby disappeared. Black velvet fur ran down the back of his legs, over his back and down his tail, turning him satin black. His chameleon coat allowed him to quickly vanish, returning to shadowland, a whispered presence so quiet we almost believed we had imagined him.

We hoped he would not stay. We didn't need another cat in our family. Our cats agreed. Larena, matriarch of our little tribe, charged Phantom with fangs and claws whenever he crossed an invisible boundary around her family. Phantom clearly thought he should stay and the other cats should leave his new home, and we were constantly treating bites and scratches.

We didn't see him much the following fall but often enough to assure us that he, in fact, had not traveled on. Our bird feeders were a powerful draw, and the presence of other cats told him this was not a threatening environment. We would have been content to let him stay as he wished, or go, but he seemed determined to interrupt our peaceable kingdom. He was always close by, sometimes resulting in unpredictable encounters.

Once upon entering our woodshed, I discovered him fearfully cowering in our woodpile. I tried to back out, but my movement caused panic, and he bolted through the closed window, breaking the glass into sharp shards. There thankfully was no sign of blood, and amazingly he seemed unharmed. We replaced the shattered pane with plywood and doubled our caution entering the many shadowed places where he might be hiding.

As fall turned to winter, we discussed what could be done to help the situation. It was clear that this wanderer was not going to wander away. He began traveling to our neighbor's farm as well, and there was talk of shooting the poor guy. He wisely returned to our safer place, and we tried to make sure he was always separated from the other cats. While the other cats ate and slept secure in the barn, we provided alternative quarters for the stray.

We wedged the door open to the shop and began putting food and water inside, along with a box filled with blankets in our little wagon. When winter winds blew snow into whirls of ice outside the shop door, we added a heat light and a heated water bowl. Heartbreakingly, the cat would run from us when we put food out, hiding under a bush near the door and crying to us as icy rain dripped down upon him and then snow. We tried to coax him to us, but his existence in the wild had deeply engrained a distrust of people. I felt he wanted to join us and was asking but was not brave enough to venture from his hiding place.

It was a sad winter, we lost one of our dear horses to colic, and so we let the wild tomcat's existence and the problems he was causing slide along, day-by-day with no solution. When the winter turned bitter cold, our acknowledgment of this mystery cat who wanted to be a distant member of our household turned to action.

I set a live trap in the shop, baited with tempting food, and when we checked, there was a very mad cat inside. He hissed and growled as I covered the trap with a blanket—useful in calming wild captured animals, my Department of Natural Resources staff and colleagues had assured me—and whisked him away to the brave veterinarian who agreed to neuter and vaccinate him. Back home we watched him carefully as he recovered from the anesthetic, making sure he had no water until he was fully conscious so there was no danger of him drowning in his water dish. When he seemed to be moving about normally, we opened the kennel and released a gray and black blur that raced away from confinement and us. All the time we had spent building trust with this wild creature seemed to have vanished with the blowing snow.

We feared he was gone forever, following the river to another place where he felt less threatened, but his vaccinations had bought him some protection and neutering would eliminate future litters of unwanted wild babies. We couldn't help checking under his bush as we walked by for evening chores and found, as we expected, no tabby hiding in the green branches. But the next morning when I walked to the barn, he was there, under his bush by the door, crying plaintive meows but not daring to come inside as I filled his dish and put fresh water in his heated bowl.

Life went on like this, with our wild cat a distant member of our cat family, until one day he wandered inside the barn where the other cats were eating and joined them, all the while keeping a watchful eye on Larena. Later, he followed the other cats upstairs into the loft where large boxes with warm blankets were positioned under heat lights and curled up among the hay bales. There he could enjoy the companionship of the other cats and benefit from the lamps as long as he remained respectful of the invisible boundary Larena had set.

And so the winter continued with our barn cats and Phantom, our new family member, spending guarded nights and days together as the snow and wind challenged all creatures outside. Perhaps it was the loneliness or watching how the other cats interacted with us, coming for pets with nothing happening to them. Perhaps they told him that we would do him no harm. For gradually, he allowed us to approach him while he nibbled his dry food. Eventually the tolerance grew to his coming to greet us for feedings, and then to rubbing on our legs, and finally to jumping up in our laps as we sat upon the bedding bags at the back of the barn. This fearful creature, this phantom cat, actually loved being scooped up in our arms and cuddled while he nuzzled tighter against us and purred his joy.

Held close in our arms, we were able to fully explore the exotic beauty of his gray and black coat, the myriad stripes and intricate spots that covered him. I never tired of looking at him and stroking his so soft fur. His had not been an easy life before coming to Leap of Faith Farm. A scar cut at an angle across his broad nose. One nostril was torn on the outside edge, and a notch in one ear testified to a hard-fought battle. When Phantom walked with us, he always trotted slightly ahead, tail curved downward over fast moving bow legs. He was as magnificently strong as he was calm and gentle.

In accepting us, Phantom finally found acceptance among the other cats. After years of fighting to survive, he had found a family and a job on the farm. He was "Provider," a fearsome hunter, a stealth machine camouflaged in dark shadows where he waited patiently for that instant when a bird turned away, a mouse darted back to pick one more seed, a vole was slow returning to his burrow. With his prey grasped tightly in massive jaws, he called out his victorious quest. And the other cats came running to him, chirping praise as they tripped along beside him, twining tails and rubbing against his flank until with great flourish, he laid the hapless victim at their feet and went a short distance away to groom and watch the feast.

Poor Phantom, when all the barn cats were gone and even he had become an indoor/outdoor cat, he would bring his trophy to our doorstep, crying loudly for everyone to come out and see the prize he had captured. Sadly, only his human family remained to praise his accomplishments. This wild cat had charmed us all—feline and human alike—and brought us his greatest offering, his trust and his love.

Soul Mates

Wild Cat
    Hides in shadows
Meows warnings
    Against feared harm

Phantom cat
    Feral, ferocious
Breaking windows
    Escaping approach

Sweet black and white Chess cat
    Seeks feline friendship
Greets hostile threats
    Tail up, whiskers twitch

Crazy twisting dance
    Aggressive   Compliant
Scratches and bites
    Unyielding enthusiasm

Then against all odds, the magic
    A heart won over
Massive strength yields
    To gentle spirit

Frantic chases gone
    Partners now
Together they hunt
    Share warm sun patches

Heads butt in greeting
    Tails intertwine
Strolling fields
    Sharing toys and mice alike

Death awaits
    Dear Chess
Time is borrowed
    Disease will win

Phantom watches
    Waits
Can he know?
    Or has he always known?

Phantom and Chess—The Odd Couple

Chess took an immediate liking to the large gray and black tabby who glared at him and hissed threats to not come closer. It seemed our little black-and-white cat desperately wanted a new companion after the disappearance of his buddy Justin and came eagerly forward to welcome the new feline. Unfortunately, his friendly overtures often ended with vicious attacks, and Larena protectively chasing Phantom away from her kitten. We stood by helplessly watching the encounters and then assessing the damage that had been done to Chess, often treating abscesses that arose on his back, his leg and his tail. Chess did not learn quickly.

With Chess safe inside the chicken coop for the treatment of his wounds, calmness reigned. Larena kept Phantom and her family under surveillance. But when Chess was healed and released, he immediately approached the stray again, tail up, eager for a face-rubbing session. He was not discouraged. On rare occasions, Phantom tolerated Chess's affection; usually he chased him. Phantom continued to torment Chess, and Larena continued the defense of her family until he was trapped, neutered, vaccinated and released.

By spring, everything was going much more smoothly among the cats in our Leap of Faith pride. Larena had very low tolerance for Phantom, but he persisted in pushing his way into the circle. She yowled at him and swiped him with her paw on occasion to remind him of his place, but generally there were few hostile encounters. Most surprising was the change in the relationship between Phantom and Chess. Phantom did not always welcome Chess's need for a brotherly head-butt, and he occasionally did stalk and chase him, but over time they became companion hunters, prowling around the pond and up into the orchard together. Chess did not follow Phantom on his hunting journeys away from the farm, but he eagerly welcomed him back, a lost friend found once again, if only missing for an hour.

Phantom seemed to feel, with all his worldly knowledge gained from years spent on his own, that he needed to protect the innocent sweet cat. They spent their days together and slept together each night. When Chess became ill and spent days away from the farm at a hospital, Phantom searched for him. When Chess returned, Phantom entered willingly in mutual grooming sessions to remove the alien medicinal smells. They walked together, tails swaying back and forth, replacing the bad smells with sweet grass and flower scents until the day we carried Chess from the barn into the garage loft, leaving only Phantom and Larena in the barn.

Phantom called continually for his friend. It was all very sad, but Chess's life was at stake. If only they could see each other every now and then. Maybe it would help their loneliness, we thought, but the logistics of arranging visits baffled us. The stairs which rose to the loft were inside our garage and encased in screen to keep bugs at bay. One day, though, we decided to try to unite the two grieving cats. Getting Phantom into the carrier went smoothly and we walked up the drive with him swinging at our side. Dick carried our hefty twelve-pound guy up the stairs and into the loft while I held Chess safely inside. When Phantom was released, they rubbed faces; then Phantom started exploring the strange human habitat with Chess following close behind. After some time they lay down together happy in each other's company once again. Leaving was easy. We opened the door and Phantom followed us down the stairs and out through the screen and garage doors to freedom.

We hadn't planned a schedule of visits, but every few days we repeated the ritual until Phantom quickly came to us for his ride to the garage and his Chess visit. After several repetitions, all we had to do was call Phantom to us and he would trot beside us to the garage, and when we opened doors for him, he climbed the stairs waiting at the loft door for entry. The visits delighted us as well as the cats. Chess's health stabilized over the winter and our solution for both cats seemed ideal. All went well until in winter's coldest time, I had a riding accident. Nic shied while I was mounting him and whirled in a circle around me, dislocating my right knee and fracturing portions of the joint. After almost a week in the hospital I went home with a cast, crutches and a walker. We called in an army of people to help Dick with chores, while I hobbled through the house and waited for spring to come and my bones to heal.

Phantom was not accepting of the strange people who fed him in his barn and the loft. Their presence was tolerated when they provided food and fresh water, but he would not follow them to visit Chess. Dick sweetly made sure that at least once a day, Phantom could follow him to the loft for a visit so the cats' friendship would continue. By spring, I could negotiate my way into the garage and up the stairs for Chess's feeding and medicine, sometimes opening the garage door so Phantom could accompany me. But my husband felt my trips to the loft were too difficult and dangerous for me, and a better plan was needed.

Early summer came. Even with air conditioning in the loft, the rooms began reaching uncomfortable levels over the hottest days. The weather, combined with my injured leg, necessitated contemplation of another move. Could we bring Chess downstairs and keep him safe in the utility and mudroom between the garage and family room? We had to try.

Introducing strange cats to each other was something very familiar to us. We started with keeping the door between Chess and our inside cats closed. Then over days, we opened it a crack to allow exchange of smells and maybe a glimpse of the cats beyond. Finally baby gates were stacked, one on top of the other, until the entire doorway was open. It was a good exposure opportunity for the cats, but a very difficult gymnastic feat for the humans who had to remove the center gate and crawl through the opening when we came in and out of the house.

Gradually the gates were taken down, except at night. Each evening before going to bed, we closed protective wooden doors to the mudroom assuring that our shy, gentle cat would have unobstructed access to his bed, water and food bowls, and litter pans. All was good for Chess and the inside cats, but what about Phantom? It took only a few trips for Phantom to transition from visiting Chess in the loft to following us into the mudroom. It seemed as we headed into fall that we had a working system that kept everyone happy and was fairly easy for us to maintain. But in the fall, everything changed once again.

Just Larena and Phantom remained in the barn that once sang with cat meows and rooster crows. Our horses were sole reminders of those earlier times; our hearts were heavy in the silence around us. Only the two cats were left to feed in the barn and snuggle under a truce beneath the heat lamps at night.

Larena was getting to be an old girl, and when we took her for a routine veterinary check, her weight loss was significant. It was during that visit that bladder cancer was discovered. Larena's days in the barn, where she had sought refuge for her family years ago, were ending. We brought her inside to live in our basement as we struggled to keep her comfortable. Now Phantom alone was left in the barn. It wasn't a hard choice—really the only option available—the last step in transitioning from barn life to an inside home. Phantom came to live inside with Chess. Every night they slept together in the mudroom. Every morning, he trotted beside us to the barn for chores and the many things on his agenda for the day. At sunset he walked beside us through the pink haze up the drive and into the garage, and then to the house where Chess waited with welcoming head butts and warm purrs.

Kasota—Down the Long Road

He was a winter cat. Pale winter moon yellow, the color of the soft yellow sandstone along the banks of the Blue Earth River in southern Minnesota. The source of his Native American name.

We heard him before we saw him as we walked down the snow encrusted drive from our home one evening. In the distance, the river rushed over rocks before disappearing beneath ice islands, the roar carrying up from the bottom land to us as we crunched our way in the Minnesota winter night. Then above it all, a cat call floated, not plaintive but demanding. "Listen," it said. "I am in need. Find me."

He found us, calling to us as he bounded up from the river and joined in our late night sojourn. We were eager to get home, to the warmth of the fire, out of the night air that created icicles on our hair and froze our faces. He was joyous, circling round his new companions. He led the way jumping in and out of snow prints, meowing a request for our touch. And so it was that he followed us to his new home at Leap of Faith Farm.

We found him in the woodshed curled into a burlap bag for warmth, and when we trekked through the snow to the barn to feed the next morning, he leaped over the surrounding snowdrifts to join us. Eager for food, he scarcely glanced at our barn cat family who amazingly permitted him to eat with them. But that was Kasota. A tiny, unassuming little feline, he instantly fit in with the others without a single hiss or paw swipe. And so he became another addition to Larena's tribe. He got along with everyone, actually he was welcomed by them. They acted as though he had always been there and belonged among them.

His favorite friend, though, was Justin, a long and lanky young male cat. Buff colored, like Kasota, the two were almost inseparable. They hunted together and strolled through the orchard, their tails intertwining with each step. Sitting side by side, they watched the birds overhead and then raced in a game of chase to the barn. Justin had a wanderlust spirit, that thankfully Kasota did not possess. He seemed content to wind in and out between our legs as we gathered apples and then sat watching as his buddy left without him, his tail waving back and forth slowly, as he descended the hill to the field and faded into the distance. Kasota did not follow, but he was overjoyed when his friend found his way home, whether a day later or a week, until the day Justin did not return.

Larena's other kittens—Chess and Jessie—didn't have the same appeal. When Justin was gone, Kasota sought out human playmates. He was not at all afraid of our two horses. He walked under and around their legs when we groomed them, and joined in when I played with them. He loved to chase the end of my lunge whip as I directed my horses in circles around me, warming them up for a ride. Fun for him, too much excitement for me, as he came ever so close to those dangerous fast-moving hooves across the sand. If I chased Kasota out of harm's way, he climbed a nearby fence post and sat studying our movements, critiquing how well we performed intricate dressage patterns, then scampered ahead of us back to the barn.

We made a deal with all the cats at Leap of Faith Farm. We agreed to feed and water and provide a warm bed for each of them, but in exchange they had to submit to neutering and spaying, annual vaccinations and tick and flea repellent applications. This young tomcat was no exception. His initial trip to the veterinary clinic set a pattern that would be repeated his entire life. Kasota hated travel. Maybe he thought we would take him somewhere and leave him as he might have been left before near our farm; maybe he felt ill from the movement of the car. We never knew. But we did know he was unhappy. He would cling to us like a tiny monkey when we tried to put him in his carrier. Once inside he cried non-stop the entire trip, both to and from the veterinary clinic. He also would stick his nose through the slots in the carrier causing his cries to take on a muffled choking sound.

Usually, veterinary trips were for routine examinations, but occasionally, someone would find themselves in an emergency situation. Kasota was tiny, but he was bold and confident. Any tomcat who ventured onto our property received a prompt and aggressive suggestion to leave at once. Sometimes, they had different ideas. One Memorial Day weekend, as we attempted to ready our garden for planting, Kasota came inside the wire fence, and lay down on his side. He didn't play with our fingers placing tiny seeds in the ground, or roll little rocks back into the smooth dirt. He just lay there. It didn't feel right.

I called the veterinary clinic and persuaded a kind soul to meet us for an emergency diagnosis. The doctor found signs of a cat fight, particularly a bite that looked suspicious. A close look at a blood sample under the microscope showed that Kasota had contracted a blood parasite from the bite that was often fatal to cats. The doctor prescribed medication and allowed us to take Kasota home, but he was very clear that if he recovered, he probably would not survive another exposure to the parasite. We took our boy home and set up care in our makeshift cat kennel, the old chicken coop, in the barn. We treated him with antibiotics, tended to his wounds, and miraculously he soon became our healthy kitty again. When the doctor released Kasota, he strongly advised that he become an indoor cat only. He was just too little to take on large tomcats and not get hurt, and another possible exposure to the parasite was too great a risk.

When he was well enough and the weather was good, we moved him from the coop to the three-season porch along the back of our house. Through open screens, he became acquainted with our inside cats—Tasha, Hallie and Dancer. There never seemed to be a dispute about his presence on the porch, so after a week or so of getting to know everyone, we held our breath, opened the door and invited him into our home. He walked in, smelled noses with everyone, and that was that. He never left us.

Kasota never lost his love for the outdoors and we constantly had to guard against his escaping. All of the cats were trained to walk on a leash outside. He loved the opportunity but hated the restriction. He would race flat out across the yard and up the nearest tree. He would climb up into the highest branches as far as his leash would allow and sit swaying with the wind as foolish birds landed near him or fluttered on the ground below. Finally, tiring of his arbor tower, he would begin the climb back down, always crying for help when he found the descent much more difficult than the climb up. At calmer times he snuggled with us in the hammock, or patrolled the yard, smelling each leaf for the scent of an intruder. Kasota never sprayed inside the house, but he put his heart into marking his territory outside. Finding strong evidence of a cat presence, he would back up to the offending plant and spray as high as he could, hopping back and forth on his hind feet. He wanted other cats to know just what kind of giant feline they were dealing with if they came on our property again.

Only once did he escape from the house. It was Christmas and packages were frequently being delivered to our front door. I had a million things on my mind as I signed for the last delivery that day. A party was planned for the evening with people arriving in just over an hour. I counted cat noses, preparing to move everyone to the basement where they would be safe—away from people, their food, and the chance they might slip out into the snow-packed night. I only counted three noses. My breath caught in my throat. I was one pink nose short. There was no Kasota. I searched everywhere, all his favorite hiding places including our towel cabinet in the bathroom. He was nowhere. Even offering his favorite treats brought no response. I had to accept that somehow he had gotten outside, probably during the last package delivery I guessed.

Making sure the other cats were securely downstairs, I grabbed my winter gear and a flashlight and started my search. The barn was closed for the night, so he couldn't have joined his friends there, but he might have tried. So I hurried through the snow, panning the flashlight beam like a light house lantern in a half circle before me. I'd almost given up when the light caught flickering green ahead to the left of the barn. There he was, huddled at the corner near his coop, almost hidden in the drifted snow. He didn't run. Maybe he was waiting for me to find him and carry him into his warm home. Back inside our cozy home, my heart calmed finally, I took a deep breath and wiped the tears from my eyes, just as the doorbell rang.

Kasota loved the snow and didn't seem at all concerned about Minnesota winters. Before he became an inside cat, he often accompanied us on our nighttime walks down our snowy road. Our drive was two thirds of a mile long, and though he frolicked along beside us on the trip away, we often carried him most of the way home. On warm winter days, I frequently took the cats for walks outside on the plowed driveway. Kasota, safely on his leash, bounded ahead down the drive. While Dancer stood on his hind legs, begging me to rescue him from the cold white stuff, Kasota dove head first into one drift after another, emerging with snow encrusted whiskers, and a smile. Snow made him happy. So did having his people to talk with and snuggle against.

Kasota didn't just meow, he carried on conversations and always wanted to have the last word. His voice was a curious quack sound like that of the Affleck Insurance duck. And each of our comments to him received a quacking response that always had us laughing.

Kasota took his role in our home seriously. He happily greeted each visitor, arching his back as their hands swept down his yellow coat, textured and warm. He entertained my friends by playing with their shoe strings or toes beneath our old table as we sat talking. He accompanied workers as they worked on projects throughout the house. While Hallie kept the other indoor cats in their place, Kasota was their friend and true leader. He was our protector. He regarded all rug fringe as a threat and would carefully walk around the edges, never across the rug. He attacked the cord on my hair dryer as if it were a twisting snake bent on biting me. No longer hunting real prey outside, he became a ferocious bird toy predator, hiding under the bed and leaping at the swirling feathers, sometimes throwing a hiss in for good measure.

He woke me each morning with his quacking meow. He rubbed noses with me and licked my face. He sat on my lap as I wrote stories and poems on my computer or prepared documents for work. He tolerated me reading a book while I held him but had no tolerance for my attention being divided between him and my iPhone. Just my picking it up was grounds for his departure. Hallie always had the dominant spot on my chest, but when she died, he snuggled inside my arm, against my heart, purring contentment or uttering guttural meows. At night in bed he tucked his cold feet against my side in the curve of my arm or wrapped his body around my head on the pillow. During long nights when I couldn't sleep, my faithful feline followed me from the couch to bed and back to the couch again, never leaving me alone with my thoughts. I bear a forever scar from Kasota, who one night frightened from a sound sleep, leaped from his under-my-chin spot and slashed my upper lip with his departing claw. I look in the mirror and smile at the faint scar, remembering my yellow cat.

Kasota always wanted to go down the road, away. On every walk at Leap of Faith Farm, and later at our home in Kansas, he would start at a slow walk and then a jog, going somewhere only he knew. I wondered if he was trying to go back to his home. It was many years before he finally did leave us. I hope he found that long road he always wanted to go down, though it would lead him out of our lives forever.

Ghost—It Must Have Been Moonglow

Halloween Eve. The full moon illuminated the white siding on our house causing an eerie glow against the black sky. Tree branches swaying in the chill air caused shadows to play across our home interrupted occasionally by windows and the warm light within. We clutched our coats tight against our chests as we hurried from the barn into the welcome heat that waited for us inside our house. Almost like an apparition, a white cat sat before us along the curve of our drive amid the rustling dry leaves of the peony bushes. Curious, watching, wondering what we would do. As we quietly approached her, the cat's bravery vanished and so did she, into the night. "Where had she gone?" we wondered. We had not so much as glimpsed a floating white tail marking her retreat into the darkness.

Probably another cat wandering through our farm on its way to hunt or to return to its home and hopefully a warm bed we thought. But it was so late in the season to be traveling through. We saw the little cat on several other nights, her white coat shining in the moonlight. And each time, she waited until we grew near and then she was gone.

Minnesota Octobers are unreliable and sometimes deadly. Nice during the day and then turning cold so abruptly, sometimes accompanied by ice and snow, the weather has historically found people dangerously unprepared. One memorable Halloween, hunters dressed for a warm afternoon were later found frozen, unable to find their way to vehicles and safety. I worried about all animals, large or small, who might be without shelter as darkness descended each October night. I feared for the white cat.

For several nights, the cat thankfully had not been at her post along our drive as we came in for the night. She had gone home, I thought, and slept peacefully free of concern for her whereabouts. Early morning, as the winter sunrise cast pink shadows across the fields, I threw on an extra layer against the cold and walked out onto the patio. There in broad daylight in front of me stood the white cat. No apparition, but a mewing feline who announced loudly she needed something.

She had been so elusive when I tried to approach her that I felt she must be feral. I was surprised when she continued talking to me, rubbing against and around my legs. "Well, Hi, girl," I greeted her. "Are you hungry?" She meowed a loud reply. Animals waited for their breakfast in the barn, but I was reluctant to leave her in the cold. I hurried into the house, grabbed some cat food and water, and opened the door into the garage, inviting her inside. Seeing bowls in hand, she didn't hesitate but trotted to me and greedily started consuming the provisions I set before her, muttering guttural meows through her purrs. I closed her in the garage and headed to the barn leaving her inside and planning how I would approach the subject of the lost little girl with my husband.

Only a few months after losing our dear Tasha, the arrival of a new cat was not what we had planned. But often times the unexpected things that came into our lives were the best things. And this little white cat, coming to us in the late fall as Hallie had many years before, seemed auspicious. We hoped she would be a very good thing in her small kitten package.

Ghost was pure white, and perfectly proportioned, like a porcelain figurine. Huge eyes, one green and one blue, dominated her slightly triangular face with a tiny pink nose at its base. Ghost, though, was no fragile flower. She was a tomboy through and through. Where Hallie's white fur always gleamed from cleanliness, Ghost's paws had a slightly dingy cast and often times there would be a smudge of undisclosed origin across the top of her head.

In contrast to all the roughness was Ghost's voice. When we picked her up, those few times she allowed us to, she never struggled, but she did comment, and her voice bleated like a lamb. We instantly thought of the popular puppet show we had grown up loving—"Shari Lewis and Lamb Chop." There was little sweetness about Ghost. She only tolerated us holding her on her terms. All the other cats had a healthy respect for the girl. She was a diva and insisted on getting her way.

Of all the cats that we had taken in, placed or adopted, none were ill with any of the many diseases that frequently plague free-ranging felines. And none came to us with fleas or other parasites. Except Ghost. She had fleas and ringworm that prevented her from being introduced to the other cats and had to be dealt with quickly. One of Ghost's earliest handling experiences was a much dreaded, on our part, bath. We debated where and when to perform the dastardly deed and settled on the large green sink in the utility room with its handy spray nozzle and the advantage of a door we could keep closed.

Into the sink went Ghost. Dick held her while I filled pitchers of warm water and gradually poured them over her. Amazingly she sat still, only offering a questioning mew. So we added shampoo, rinsed and then towel-dried the little cat. There were no hisses, swipes, bites. And she was done, looking more like a white rat than our beautiful Ghost. Thankfully, we had all survived.

Ghost loved fresh water, begging for it almost as eagerly as she did meals. When we placed a clean bowl before her, she quickly lapped a few sips with her tiny pink tongue, then sat beside the bowl and carefully dipped one front paw into the liquid, raised it to her mouth and licked it away. She repeated the unique habit until she finally had enough and walked away to groom any stray drops from her whiskers. The other cats never seemed to mind her water play but we changed water frequently to make sure it stayed clean.

Always full of energy, Ghost would try to engage a brother or sister in a game of chase or hide and seek. But she was perfectly capable of playing all parts on her own. Stiff-legged with fuzzed tail she would hop sideways, then laying ears flat she would race through the house. Sometimes she landed on the couch where she would roll about in a frenzy, coming to rest on her back with her butt propped against cushions high in the air. From this inverted stance she would throw herself wildly at strips of paper or feather toys, sometimes mistakenly or deliberately grabbing fingers or a hand instead. A stern "Ghost!" and she repented immediately, licking us instead to show it had all been a mistake.

Bathrooms fascinated Ghost. She would dive behind shower curtains, tripping lightly along the edge of the tub. She was mildly interested in what her humans did there while sitting idly below the water, but became fully engaged in tapping her paws at fingers waved enticingly through soap bubbles. She did not drink from dripping faucets as our other white cat Hallie had done, but she did help us dry ourselves after a shower, running her rough tongue over our bare feet and between our toes. Ghost demanded to be wherever we were, hooking a paw under the door and pulling until we opened it for her to join us. Two minutes later she pulled on the door again so we would open it for her to leave.

Cabinet doors she mastered on her own, pawing at the edge until she could gain entry. Frequently she only briefly explored the dark interior, but one cabinet with towels inside, she claimed as her own. Pulling them into a rough nest, she would circle and then snuggle into them for a nap. We often couldn't find her, worried, calling everywhere till finally we opened another tightly closed door, and found her sleeping on fleece blankets inside.

Ghost was a welcoming party of one when we returned from the barn and began the lengthy process of changing out of our heavy Carhartt overalls and jackets into house clothes. She wound in and around our legs, compounding the instability that always threatened to send us sprawling as we changed. Following this she would stretch out on her side, somewhere dangerously close to our moving feet, and begin bathing herself. She spent considerable time licking a back foot and then used it to wash her face, first rubbing along her cheeks then over an ear. We would pet her and tell her how much we appreciated her help until she decided she had done enough and wandered away.

It took a long time for her to agree to sit with us. She preferred to find a favorite blanket on the couch, kneading it to perfection before settling down. More commonly she would find a bed already warmed by another cat. Sometimes she would begin with soft licking to encourage her fellow cat to move on and let her have her rightful spot. Often she would stare at the interloper, her pupils enlarging into what we referred to as "the stink eye," daring them to remain. If all else failed she would attack and the hapless blanket holder would leave. Perhaps she was only following the behavior she had observed in our horses. Some trainers believe that horses exert dominance by getting other horses to move their feet, and maybe she saw the wisdom in applying that approach to the other cats. It seemed to work well for her unless we intervened.

Frequently her aggressive strategy was all for nothing as we put her down or sent her spilling off the blanket onto the floor, grumbling her objection as she left. In a short time she would return, seeking her favorite people furniture—my ankles crossed to form a little hammock, just Ghost size. Another favorite sleeping spot was on top of my feet as I lay on the couch beneath a warm blanket reading.

She cried loudly for food, giving her little lamb bleats until a full bowl appeared before her. Sometimes she was really hungry, sometimes she just loved putting her humans through the exercise. She would sit on the rug waiting for her bowl, posing with her left paw raised like a Chinese good luck cat. "Are you hungry, Ghost?" we asked. "Baaa," she mewed. Down came the dish before her. After taking three bites, she walked away waving her tail. "We don't run a deli here," my husband would tell her. But then we'd do it all over again. We were so well trained.

Our cats were rarely given people food—maybe a small piece of tuna or salmon occasionally—but generally nothing. Ghost was the exception. I would sit with my plate watching TV and she would approach, first from one direction, then another. I'd suggest she leave but she bounced back until I offered a tiny quarter inch piece of cheese, the prize she was after. And then she would leave. Yogurt was another matter. From another floor in our house, she could hear my husband softly peeling back the cover on a yogurt container and seconds later she would be there before him, purring and rubbing against his legs. Sometimes the girl had to get more insistent. Sitting on the table before him she gently tapped his hand until he offered a taste of yogurt to her on his spoon. Then off she would go, content again.

Ghost never seemed interested in leaving her inside home once she was there, although she enjoyed walking outside with us just as the other cats did. They all wanted to explore; she wanted to investigate. Every leaf she encountered merited a careful nose sniff for information. Every branch required a cheek rub from its base to the tip. She could never pass by a sunny patch on the gravel drive without dropping to her side and rolling luxuriously back and forth till her white fur became dusty yellow. Ghost was the cat we waited on. The others strained to the extent of their leashes while we patiently encouraged her to come along. Only trees motivated action. After clawing the bark for a moment or two, she climbed as high as she could, limited in her ascent only by a collar and a restricting line. She embraced the outside world.

The little white imp bewitched us. She could be a challenge. Nail trimming was not for the weak of heart as she meowed her objection and suggested a bite was not far away. But brushing was something she loved and sat quietly as we smoothed her often ruffed, short, white coat. And if we scratched the top of her little head, she lifted it up into our palms, eyes closed and purring contentment with love for us. It was hard not to love our rare lunar girl in return. It must have been moon glow that led us straight to her.

PART 3: Heart Horses

CHAPTER 5:
Horses Come From Heaven

A good non-horse friend, understanding my love for horses, gave me the soft yellow sweatshirt with the words that always began the conversations—"Horses Come From Heaven." "Are you a horsewoman?" strangers asked me at the doctor's, office, the grocery store, yoga class; no matter where I was, we began sharing stories of the horses in our lives. My husband has always said, "They're everywhere," though that is not true. Loving horses, I believe, is in the DNA of those of us that breathe the smell of horses like we breathe air. And we can't imagine life without them.

Heart Horses appear in our lives to gift us with their presence. They touch us deep inside and we are forever influenced by their soft eyes, strength, gentleness and beauty. They test our constancy and patience and sometimes our bravery, our capacity for joy and the depth of our sorrow.

Over the years before coming to Leap of Faith Farm and during our time there, I was blessed by five of the wondrous beings. I never wanted a herd of horses. I treasured each animal as an individual that I could build a relationship with over their lifetime.

I never understood the attitude of horse owners who saw their equines as a means to an end, trading them like vehicles for newer and better models until they were eventually cast aside with no reverence for all their horses had given them. My horses were my horses for life, no matter what happened to them and what they needed. They didn't ask to be in my life, and I treasured my responsibility to them.

I felt a special connection to all my horses. They were unique individuals with their own thoughts and emotions. They brought immeasurable joy to my life and hopefully they felt I took good care of them. I learned from each of them to be a more skilled horse person and a better person. I will always be grateful to my Heart Horses.

Dunny Money—The Good Day

It was not so much that he actually spoke to me. The thought simply came into my mind as I led my old friend from his stall that early spring day. Gray clouds, which enveloped the farm for days and cried rain that drew frost from the ground and left mud behind, had blown away overnight. Now bright blue sky remained. A gentle breeze lifted Dun's mane and ruffled my hair as we walked together down the path to the sand arena out behind the barn. This was a day of promises after a long Minnesota winter and the difficulties of caring for our aging fellow who had been separated from his dominant pasture mate, Lars, and housed inside the pole barn for many months.

And yet I heard the words so clearly. "Today is a good day to die." That is what he said to me. So, when Dick returned from his usual Saturday morning trip to Good Thunder for a paper and supplies and told me that Dun was lying down in the arena, it was as if I had been waiting all morning for the moment.

Lars, his pasture buddy, stood in the dry lot anxiously watching his friend in the far corner of the arena, struggling to rise. I watched too for a moment and then recalled all the sage wisdom about down horses and colic and the need to get them up and moving. What had happened that had sent this day spinning downward?

Last night Dun had been eager to come inside to the warmth and comfort of his stall, his home for the last eight years. He had eaten all his feed the night before. Yes, there had been some grain left from his morning feeding, but as the weather improved, Dun sometimes left it uneaten in his eagerness to get outside to his hay. I'd scolded him slightly for peeing in his stall moments before leading him out, my patience drained by the end of another week and tiredness setting in. He'd hung back in the corner watching me, waiting to see if I was past my momentary anger and had forgiven him. All this haunted me as I helped my gelding struggle to his feet. I listened for gut sounds, assurance that his digestive system was functioning, but sounds were indistinct. Gums seemed moist, not tacky, but how could I be sure? And their color always seemed pale.

Exasperated by my lack of action, Dick urged me to call the vet. Again the wisdom, "Keep him moving," I called to Dick as I raced for the phone. Our usual equine veterinarian was on another call, but his staff agreed to alert him and assured us he would come as soon as possible. Back by Dun's side again, it seemed like such a long time to keep a 1000-pound animal taking tiny steps. I was doubtful that we could keep our end of the bargain as I watched his hindquarters swaying threateningly to one side and then the other. I told him what a good boy he was…just a little longer, just keep moving. And dear obedient Dun plodded patiently at my side.

When my veterinarian arrived, he quickly assessed the situation and told us that, as we feared, Dun had colic. He quickly administered the usual Banamine and mineral oil telling us that we needed to decide if we wanted to ship him to the University of Minnesota Veterinary Hospital and, if we waited, the trip might not be possible. Watching Dun staggering and his eagerness to lie down, I thought it was already too late. And so we gambled that a miracle would happen, that it was best to keep him at the farm with us rather than risking his possible fall in route to St. Paul or dying at the University. It seemed we made the right choice. We all sighed and remarked on the close call as Dun trotted off to stand nose-to-nose with his buddy munching hay along the fence.

Two hours later, he was pacing. Another visit from our veterinarian who stated the inevitable "nothing more to be done." He left additional pain medication with us, just in case Dun became more uncomfortable. He suggested that we keep him in the pole barn where he could move around, but I knew he was worried my horse might go down in his stall and we would not be able to move him from it. Then he said very softly, "If this old guy wants to lie down and rest, let him; he's earned it."

By evening the bright day was gone and rain had started to fall. Poor Dun, alone in the pole barn after all his warm cozy nights tucked next to Lars in his stall—the stall I always promised he would have one day, along with the green pasture and acres to roam, the cool shade trees and apples to nibble from the orchard. I gave it all to him; it just wasn't long enough. That night, we left Lars outside in the lean-to so he could keep watch over his friend. But, instead of standing inside, he maintained vigil at the fence line, as close to Dun as he could get.

We put blankets on them both and went inside for a restless few hours. By ten when we checked, Dunny's blanket was wet with sweat. He staggered restlessly around the barn, wandering aimlessly. He seemed to be searching for a way out, away from the barn, the situation, from us. He would not be comforted by our words or our hugs. I decided to administer another shot to ease the pain, a decision that has haunted me. For though I've given many shots and know the protocol, I did not pull back to test for blood before pushing the Banamine into his body. Perhaps he was only reacting to the pain he felt deep inside somewhere we could not touch, but he seemed to shudder and then backed away from us continuing his endless circles. Reluctantly, I followed Dick back to the house to wait through the long night until morning. I have regretted not spending that night with him in his torment, but I did not. While he searched for his way away, I stayed inside waiting and fearing morning.

With the morning came the truth that our Dun was gone. He lay on his side in the sand where he had once made circles beneath me, riding round and round in our schooling together. It was Easter Sunday, just three days short of his thirtieth birthday. A nearby neighbor offered to help bury our dear horse at the spot we had selected beneath his beloved apple trees.

Snow fell in great flakes the next day. Dick had to leave for an out-of-state meeting planned before our tragedy at Leap of Faith. Dun lay under a blue tarp in the chilled arena. We had said goodbyes and brought Lars to visit his friend one last time. Lars nickered to Dun, nudging his nose with this muzzle, urging him to come play. But there was no response, and he gradually walked away.

Later, Lars and I stood in the barn. We couldn't watch as our neighbor lifted Dun and carried him from the arena along the run and through the snow up into the orchard. They laid him gently there in the still frozen dirt. Such a huge hole, and still not large enough somehow for such a great animal. I gave them his blue blanket to cover him, his halter for remembrance, a wreath of pine and cedar from the yard, and apples and carrots tied with a ribbon for his journey. And finally, close to his nose so he would not forget me, I tossed my old hat. The hat he loved to snatch from my head and toss far down the barn aisle.

I asked them to cut a shank of his tail so that I could keep a little of my Dun with me. Neighbors and friends sent cards and brought flowers for me, and carrots for Lars. Gradually, grass grew over Dun's grave and a new monument rested there. Ribbons, and pictures, and a shaft of black tail hair adorned with silver, remain, along with emptiness from the loss of that great little horse, and almost twenty-five years of memories.

The beginning of our journey together, however, started many years before when my dad bought my first horse, a Quarter Horse mare named Taffy Brown—a dream horse for the little girl who always loved horses more than anything. During grade school and high school Taffy and I were constant companions. I had only ridden my sweet mare occasionally during the years I was away at college, so I understood the decision to sell her to someone who would care for her, but my heart was broken. I was not there the day she was wrapped in a bright blue sheet and traveled away to her new home, whinnying good-byes.

Her new owner bred Taffy over the next few years, and she produced several foals. I was not aware that my father had made a deal with Taffy's buyer that I could pick any of her babies to own. When he told me of the deal he had made and that a horse was waiting for me in Kansas, I was thrilled. I visited Taffy and her offspring on one of my trips home. All her babies were beautiful, but my choice was made the minute I saw Dunny Money, a burnished golden dun, complete with black mane and tail, a dorsal stripe running down his back, and zebra-striped legs. He was a more masculine version of my dear Taffy, eye-catching, athletic and huggable, a perfect blend. And the large gentle eye with its arched brow that I would forever search for in future horses as an indicator of a good horse.

Dun stayed in Kansas, and I made arrangements for a nearby

family to care for him and begin his training. I planned to have him moved to Lexington where I was teaching at the University of Kentucky in a short time. In the meantime, the teenage girl who would be working with him agreed to write to me about his progress and send pictures. At first, the news was good; he was coming along nicely, although he seemed lethargic. The pictures that accompanied her letter, however, shocked me. Ribs plainly showed through Dun's golden hide, and a ridge along his topline was evident. The girl and her father argued that it was just his breeding. I insisted it was clear that he was being starved. In the end, I gave up on the training and had him moved to my uncle's farm with cattle for companions and good green grass filling his belly and rounding his frame once again.

Dun never lived in Kentucky. I had met someone whom I thought I would love forever. We commuted through a relationship for almost a year, traveling between Kentucky and Minnesota where he lived. Finally, I moved to Minneapolis. And Dun came with me from Kansas to Minnesota. We rented a tiny one-horse trailer and had a hitch installed on the back of my dad's car. We put a bucket of grain on the floor in the trailer, Dun hopped in and away Mom and Dad, Dun, my fella and I went. But red flags quickly appeared during our eight-hour trip north. My guy did not drive slowly enough for a towing vehicle, especially with my darling horse inside the trailer behind. I worried and complained throughout the trip. All of us made it safely to Minnesota, but by spring, the guy was gone and the horse stayed. Shortly afterwards, my future husband entered my life.

Dun was only five when he came to Minnesota. I had not ridden in quite a few years. So, we learned a lot about each other. My smart little guy always tried to guess what I wanted before I asked. And he was not happy about being corrected. He was strong under saddle, and I often came home in tears, sobbing to Dick that I would have to sell Dun because he was just too much horse for me.

Dun tried to out-think my wishes and then became worried when he guessed wrong. His willfulness, which included bouts of running away with me early in our time together, led me to wishing for more control and harsher aids. I was leaning strongly in that direction after some frightening encounters when I fortunately moved to a new boarding place, and the owner convinced me that dressage, training that relies upon the relationship and communication between horse and rider to execute patterns and movement using very subtle direction, might be the answer that I had been searching for as a peaceful way to work effectively with my opinionated fellow. And so we schooled for hours in circles and shoulders-in and half passes. Blue ribbons and complete faith in a simple snaffle bit later, we had resolved our differences, and I relied completely upon the little horse. He was not the typical competitor with his 14.2 hand foundation Quarter Horse frame, short legs, and sturdy build. But Dunny put his heart into everything he did, and his long body allowed great flexibility that delighted the instructors, making him a very good dressage horse.

I loved dressage, and fortunately Dun found the test patterns challenging enough to keep him interested. When we started competing, people would look in amazement as I entered the arena on the heels of a tall lanky thoroughbred. But we frequently left with ribbons and comments about his even gait and bend. Natural horsemanship was ideal training for Dunny's intelligent mind. He learned voice commands, followed me without any lead, and when working at liberty he careened to a halt and came to me with one short whistle.

There were health issues that we worked to overcome and that haunted us both during Dun's entire life. At his first stable in Minnesota, the owners unfortunately stored their hay at one end of their indoor arena. Everyday dust from riders and their horses settled into the green foliage and was consumed by the hungry horses. Dun became very ill with a respiratory infection. He recovered but was diagnosed with heaves, an equine emphysema that had to be managed all his life. Muggy summer days found him standing with his head down trying to expel air from his compromised lungs. He had to be stabled outside and fed in ways that would reduce all dust. We learned to work around bad days and enjoy all the good days.

Our competition days looked as though they might end one day when the barn where he was being stabled called. Dunny had put a foot over a low fence wire and had stood pawing in frustration from not being able to graze with the other horses. His pawing had resulted in the wire cutting deeply into the back of his foot and necessitating an emergency trip to the University of Minnesota Equine Hospital. At the hospital, the doctors slowly debrided damaged tissue from his foot and wrapped it carefully. He spent many weeks in recovery at the hospital, too long for my imaginative horse. Dunny had always been bored with enclosures and often devised distracting entertainment when he was confined to a stall—switching light switches on and off with his nose, upsetting barrels within reach, and grasping loose ropes and halters with his teeth. At the hospital he learned to open his stable door. Staff arriving one morning found him wandering the barn aisle and other stall doors standing open. His escapade earned him a plaque that read: "Warning—Houdini. Double latch all doors."

Multiple surgeries at the University of Minnesota and creative farriering over many months led to his recovery. But, because of his injury, the back quarter of his foot eventually had to be amputated. The hoof wall never grew correctly again. Veterinarians were skeptical that I would ever be able to ride him again. But I was determined to work with him until he was well again. And I did ride him and compete with him many more years. During his recovery, I wrote an article about his injury for Equus magazine to help inspire other horse owners not to give up in the face of their horse's injuries and illnesses. I also was asked to test and become a spokesperson for a new medical product designed to stimulate skin growth that would eventually be used for burn victims. Many good things came from such a bad experience for Dunny and me.

Dunny loved going places. We frequently trailered to nearby trails and sometimes overnight trail rides. He raced up sandy hills, bush-wacked his way through woods, crossed streams, once stepping over me as I bent down near the bank. We swam in lakes together with me clutching tightly to his slippery hide, my hands grasping his long mane. He would do anything for his girl.

We had been through so many things together. The devastating injury to his foot followed not only his ongoing battle against heaves, but also a diagnosis of Cushing's Disease. This growth of the pituitary gland causes many easily identifiable symptoms today, but at that time were not well-known. His long wavy coat that would not shed in the spring, his thickened neck and round belly led me to ask my veterinarian to test him. He was the first case they had seen, and he was forever afterwards known at the clinic as the Cushing's horse. Treatment was not readily available at the time, but the veterinarian injected huge slow-release capsules into his chest. We clipped his coat in the summer to keep him comfortable, and we continued to love him. He did well for a long time. But there was clearly a change in his stamina and energy levels.

It was hard for both of us, the change in our relationship. For so many years, I relied on Dun. He carried me on long trail rides and amazed everyone with the elegance of his dressage movements.

Our life together changed as he grew older. My trust in him gradually faded as he became less sure of his footing. Perhaps it was lack of sensation in that bad foot that he had camouflaged for so long but could no longer hide. Occasional stumbles and trips became more frequent. A rider who loses confidence in her horse sets off a chain reaction of decline in their relationship. My fear of a bad fall led me to become tense on Dun's back. He became more unsure and hesitant. When other people rode Dun, not as aware of the changes as I was, he was much more relaxed, a different horse. I knew he was trying his best, but I worried, watching for errors as though they were deliberate. The joy I always found being with him slowly eroded away. Still, he forgave me again and again, as if to say, "She's just a human after all." He continued to look at me with those bright eyes and the pricked-up fox ears; he nickered a greeting to me each day urging me to bring his feed quicker. How could I not always love this generous intelligent creature?

It was a very sad day when my veterinarian told me the time had come to stop riding Dun. He worried that he would throw me during a bad stumble, and so our lives together changed. I exercised Dun by walking him or from Lars's back, but never again upon him. I knew we could not expect to keep him for long after that time. Dun was all about work and doing joyfully what he was asked. He was not about idleness.

It was hard to watch as he began to fail. There were more stumbles and falls. It never seemed to bother him very much. One spring day, as Lars and he galloped the length of the pasture at Leap of Faith Farm, he slipped on the wet grass, sliding along the fence and ending up with all four feet sticking through the vinyl-wrapped wire. Without panic about being too close to the fence to get his feet under him, he turned his head to the side and nibbled dandelions. He waited patiently as Dick and I frantically located a thick rope, pulled him away from the fence, and then flipped him over so he could stand. Later in the winter he fell again after a chase game. He went down near the water tank in mud so slippery he couldn't gain enough traction to stand. In usual calm quiet Dunny fashion, he rested while we rocked him on his side and placed hay bales against his back. We sprinkled shavings under his feet, and while I pulled his halter, Dick heaved against his hip, and Dun finally lunged to his feet. We decided we had to separate the two horses. Lars just wanted to play, but Dun couldn't keep up with the younger horse, so the two buddies parted. On cold days, Dun was kept inside the pole barn.

It was hard to believe that just two days ago, we had walked down the long drive to the road together, me on Lars, Dun leading the way at the end of the lead rope through the muddy tracks. Last weekend, Dick and I walked behind him through the melting snow in the hay field. We drove him on long lines in circles and serpentines as he gaily trotted ahead of us throwing up wisps of snow with each stride.

His aging had gone like that, deceptively slowly, but always downhill. And yet it was his heart that kept him going and kept asking his tired legs on that bright spring day to take one more step for his girl. And now the trail had ended.

Trails End

All week I've followed
Parallel tracks made in soft mud
On a warm afternoon
Such a little while ago

There is the circle
Where we turned and headed home
Sun glowing red
Over greening gray grass fields

You knew the way
Walking bravely ahead
Stretching lead line taut
Lars and I keeping pace

Today ice tears fell
On your still shaggy coat
White snowflakes blown by cold wind
Under ruffled caramel

Treads tear rough tracks
Through quiet white
Carrying my friend to still frozen ground
Amid bare apple trees

A blanket Long worn
Halter Faded blue
Grain and hay for your journey…away
My cap tossed alongside…with you

You know the way
We cannot follow
The trail has faded, hoof prints blend
Under snow and spring rain

Lars—Fly without Wings

My farrier stood leaning on the fence as I worked my nineteen-year-old Quarter Horse Dunny Money. I finished lunging and whistled for Dun to come to me so his hooves could be trimmed. His many injuries over the last few years meant challenges in trimming and shoeing him.

"You need a new horse," my farrier at last delivered his comment. I was about to argue how sound Dunny was when he added, "It's like chasing your grandpa around in circles."

No words came forth from my mouth. My farrier had a point. Dun was far from retirement at the time, but his periodic bouts with heaves and recovery from serious injuries had taken a toll on my boy. I couldn't expect him to continue to perform as he had forever. So I began visiting with Dun about the possibility of a new horse becoming part of his herd.

My friend and owner of the farm where I was boarding Dun was excited about the idea of a new horse for me and very willing to help with the search. She searched the internet, and we traveled miles looking for the right match—young with some sense, trained for riding, personable and with the wonderful large eye and arched eyebrows I associated with kindness. Surprisingly I found my future partner almost in my backyard. A dressage trainer at a nearby stable had a five-year-old Anglo-Arab/ Swedish Warmblood for sale. I hadn't anticipated the Arabian and Thoroughbred bloodlines of my would-be dressage horse, but I couldn't wait to set up a date to visit him at the stable.

Lars radiated quality: from his gracefully arched neck, down his long legs, to sound feet. He was simply beautiful—a brilliant red chestnut with two white socks on his back legs and a blaze down the center of his face. The trainer set him loose in the arena and urged him forward with a flick of his whip. Lars pranced proudly extending each leg. His tail was adrift in flag formation. When he stopped, he blew loud snorts and turned his head in profile. Only then did I see the large bump on his nose that partially explained why he was for sale. "A run-in with the hay rack," the trainer explained. "Just cosmetic," he assured me. But in competitive dressage circles, the blemish was not desirable. Not a problem for me. I had already fallen in love, though I did have misgivings about riding this fire-breathing beast.

The trainer saddled and rode Lars at all gaits and, as advertised, he had lovely movement. When I rode him for the first time, it was magic. I was used to Dunny's short strides and this guy was all about stretching forward and floating. "He likes you," the trainer sang out. "I have to work like the devil to get him to work for me. He likes your touch." It may not have been true, but it was what I longed to hear, and in a few days I bought him.

We competed in local dressage shows and I trained with my dressage trainer. In between shows, I practiced or took him to one of the nearby parks for trail rides. Dick sometimes came with me astride Dunny as I rode Lars. Lars was a kind, fun, and talented horse, but he was young and not always dependable. When my parents visited, my father, knowing Lars was one quarter

Thoroughbred, urged me to "Run him, run him." On the way back to the barn, I could hardly stop the massive sixteen-and-a-half hands-tall machine of a horse. We progressed steadily in his training but there were always problems that would come up, often right before a show. For several months he began grabbing the bit in his teeth, raising his head and galloping forward with me fighting for control. At other times we would begin quietly, but shortly into the ride I would glance down to see Lar's tongue flopping out the side of his mouth. He somehow managed to get his tongue over the bit and couldn't put it back in a more comfortable position.

"I wouldn't take him to a show," my trainer advised after one discouraging training session, but I went anyway. Lars was a different horse at shows. He loved all the attention we found there and sometimes there were added benefits. As I walked him into the arena in preparation for our class at one show, we stopped to visit with a man eating an ice cream cone outside the entrance gate. We were having a good conversation until Lars reached forward and, with his long pink tongue licked the ice cream off the man's cone.

Lars was excited at shows, and I was nervous, always looking for ways to calm our show-time jitters. The problem was solved when Dick accompanied us. As I hurried around getting our schedule and my competition number, he stood beside my horse making little light circles on Lar's forehead and neck until his head dropped in relaxation. Some deep breathing on my part and he and I began our test more calmly.

Judges routinely added comments about Lar's potential, and we often walked away with ribbons. Other riders commented on how nice it must be to have a horse that would stand quietly by the trailer munching hay in between classes while their horses pawed and paced in place. It's quite common to give dressage horses informal names, but I thought he needed something that better suited such an elegant animal. He was Lars at home, but at the shows the name on the registration forms was Grand Larsony for his ability to often steal the show.

Early in our relationship, to help Lars become more familiar with the sights and sounds of horse shows, I took him just for the new experience. He was gentle but sometimes, like any horse, he would decide not to do something, such as getting into the trailer. At one show, after walking around the grounds, I decided to leave, and he thought not. He planted his large feet and wouldn't budge. Friends who met us there helped encourage him to load but, even though my trailer was designed for large horses, it looked as though his giraffe neck and upright head would not clear the opening. "He's a tall glass of water," my friend commented. He was, in fact, very tall and narrow. I was always amazed how thin his neck seemed compared to my more rounded Quarter Horse.

My big red horse was all about movement. When we trotted down the road, he preferred slow collected canters. When we cantered, he preferred fast. It took a combination of closing my reins and squeezing with my legs to put him in a more manageable frame, but then he was perfect.

While we searched for a farm in southern Minnesota, we left our horses behind boarded at my friend's farm. When we located temporary housing, before the snows began, we brought them south to a boarding facility about one half hour away. They were close enough I could visit and ride them frequently, but I wanted them to be with us at our yet to be found farm. I was jubilant when we signed the contract for Leap of Faith Farm, but much needed to be done before they could be moved to their new home. Finally, after work crews had redesigned our barn and put up miles of safe white fencing, we brought them home to the pastures, and grass, and cozy clean stalls I had always promised them.

All of the knowledge I gained over many years of boarding and reading about horse care, I applied to the care of our boys in their new home. They played outside all day and came into stalls every night. I stood outside their stalls in the twilight, breathing in the horse and barn smells. I could hardly believe that there before me in my own barn was my old friend Dunny, and beautiful Lars who took my breath away whenever I looked at him.

There were few opportunities for showing in southern Minnesota. And I had very little time to spare in my new job to travel to shows. We went to clinics when they were offered and rode in schooling shows at the barn where we had boarded them. I found dressage trainers who would come to the farm for lessons. Mostly my horses and I continued to learn on our own, strengthening communication between us and enjoying each other.

From our barn we could ride the one-mile blocks of gravel roads that surrounded the farm. There were trails across fields down to the Cobb River. We gained permission from neighboring farmers to ride across Conservation Reserve Program lands, planted to native vegetation as an alternative to row crops. We could ride for hours and never have to trailer anywhere. Originally we owned ten acres of land occupied by our house, outbuildings and pastures. Gradually, we acquired another ten acres. The first acre by the house we planted in native grasses and flowers. The rest of the acreage was a hayfield that yielded wonderful soft fragrant hay. We put up enough in our loft every year for our horses and gave the rest to the farmer who cut and baled the hay for us.

Most wonderful about the hayfield was riding in it. In the spring we rode through fluttering wings of Monarch butterflies. In late summer, clouds of dragonflies followed us. We cantered in summer evening twilight through twinkling fireflies. And in winter, snow thrown from flying hooves shimmered in the pink light of sunset.

Lars and Dunny were best friends, always together until for Dun's safety, we separated them. Still, they were near to one another and could touch and talk to each other. But then one day Dun was gone. It was just Lars and me. I loved riding my warmblood in the arena and around the farm, but I hesitated to take my powerful horse out alone, relying instead on my dependable and safe Dunny. Without Dun, I began to turn more to Lars as my everything horse. And in relying on him, I gained confidence in him.

We were doing fine together, but Lars was alone most of the time. The only solution seemed to be another horse. And fortunately, we found him quickly through a dressage friend. Raider was a darling boy that I thought would be a good horse for Dick to ride and fun for me as well. He was closer to Lars's age and the two horses had a great time racing each other up the runs into the pastures. In quieter times, they stood with noses close, or with their heads draped over the other's neck, chewing the itchy spots on each other they couldn't reach on their own.

Twenty-one doesn't seem old. I always thought of Lars as being my young horse. I never thought of him as aging, as having joints that could not carry his weight as they used to, as failing to recover from injuries and illnesses. Time is the true assessor of physical health. That fall, when Dick and I returned from a trip, my animal caretaker told me Lars seemed to have trouble stepping up into the lean-to one evening. I told myself he would be fine. But he wasn't, ever again.

We could never pin-point the location of the problem in his hind leg. Stifle joint issue, the vet thought. We tried so many things: joint lubricants and injections that promised full recovery, but they all failed to bring Lars's mobility back or rekindle his spirit. I rode and he would move normally for a while, and then he became lame again. We would rest him, and his lameness disappeared, but it was never really gone. It was just lurking there when we sighed relief, waiting for the next misstep that would cause him pain again. My veterinarian recommended not riding him until there was consistent improvement in his lameness.

Lars didn't adjust to not being ridden or playing as he had with Raider. He was depressed. My veterinarian scolded me for not doing more work with him in hand. He told me the horse he was seeing wasn't Lars. I tried very hard to work with him more. We took him on more walks down the long drive beside the Cobb River all that fall. Sometimes Dick and I both walked with him, a chain lead on each side to control his exuberant spirit.

He did seem to be doing better. Then one day on a solo walk with him, my foot slid on the gravel and I stumbled and fell dropping the lead line. Escape, Lars thought. Freedom! He spun away from me across the rough plowed field, finally stopping beside Raider near the back pasture.

He was not damaged as much as we feared. He just never got any better. When winter came that year, a terrible sinus infection invaded my lovely horse. The veterinarian prescribed hot and cold compresses and antibiotics. Although the infection gradually went away, Lars continued to look ill. His coat was rough. His lovely neck grew thick. There was no light in his eyes.

February, and snow was piled deep around the barn. Lars browsed through hay outside as I worked Raider in the indoor arena, coming now and then to visit with us. Something about him seemed wrong. I watched from astride Raider as Lars first lay down in one spot and then rose and trotted to another spot to lie on the ground again. He was restless and seemed in pain. I quickly put Raider away and called the veterinarian. When he arrived, we did all of the usual things to ward off colic, to make it go away. It did, but something more terrible took its place.

Ulcers were not widely understood in horses at the time. Testing procedures were not readily available, but fortunately my veterinarian had just gotten the testing equipment needed for a diagnosis. Lars, he discovered, had a hind gut ulcer. The problem was treatment for it. My veterinarian told me to grind up every Zantac I could find and administer the medicine orally to reduce the acid in his digestive system to hopefully alleviate the pain. We did as he directed. We watched; we hoped. But in the morning, I still had a very sick horse.

We began to ready the trailer for the long trip to the nearest veterinary hospital. Iowa State, a long two hours away, was the best choice. They stood ready to receive my poor boy, but he never got there. We could not load him in the trailer. He just couldn't make it up the ramp.

Instead, Lars followed me back into the barn only to collapse in obvious pain outside his stall. He struggled to get to his feet, but his long legs would not support him. In tears I called my veterinarian. "I'll be there as soon as I can, dear," he tried to reassure me. But by the time he arrived, Lars was gone, his beautiful head with its white blaze, pink nose, and arched eye resting in my lap. A ruptured intestine was the cause. Lars was buried by kind neighbors in the apple orchard next to his dear Dunny beneath a stone that says simply, "Fly without Wings, My Friend."

On a Winter Breeze

How did you find
    That brief shiningly warm day
In all of cold Minnesota winter
    To leave me?

A moment to leave
    A lifetime of copper brilliance
Unexpected as warm chinook breezes
    For a whisper in time
    You were mine.

Horse of childhood dreams
    With grace and beauty
That took my breath away.
    How did you find me to love you?

"He likes you," the trainer said
    "He goes to work with your soft touch."
You challenged me
    Made me the best that I could be.
    Did I do enough for you?

Though it's been a while
    I feel beneath me
The power of your gait
    Flying without wings across
    Prairie grasses.

Your neck arched just so
    Cadenced and poised
Tracing patterns
    'Cross miles of soft arena dirt.

A glimpse of the deep eyes
    The gently arched brow I searched for
The white edge
    That gave others pause.

In your play, talent
    I rarely coaxed from you
Extended trots, piaffe, passage
    Dancing with your shadow
    Through sun-dappled river valley pastures

Great Horse
    Puppy of a horse
With neck hugs for me in the mornings
    Soft breaths of greeting on my face
    My equine soulmate

Now you've gone
    Wisely refusing to load
For the long journey south that might have saved you
    Asking instead to die at home near dear Raider
With warm hands on your face
    Tears falling on your bright coat

Travel well, Beloved
    Find friends who have gone before
Race with tail held high, nostrils flaring
    Across the Rainbow Bridge
    But never far from my heart.

Raider—A Girl's Got to Have a Little Pony

Lars and I were lonely. The morning rides before work did not fill the emptiness created by the death of our old friend Dun. Muddy trails firmed and the branches we passed on the way to the river now hinted at green. The white blossoms of bloodroot appeared among new shoots of grass. Time had passed almost unnoticed.

On a whim, I sent out a call to my small collection of horse friends. "I'm starting to look around for a new horse," I told them. "I'd like a good sound trail horse about fifteen or so that Dick can ride too." I really missed the rides he and I had taken since moving to the farm—me on Lars, him on dependable Dunny. There were so many places to ride just down our drive or across the fields.

Almost immediately I heard from someone who had given me dressage lessons with Lars. She told me she had recently purchased some really nice horses from a couple who lived just a short distance away. They had some others she thought I should look at. I wanted a new horse, but still the anxiety settled in. Maybe I shouldn't look. I still had Lars. A new horse is always an experiment; you never really know what you are getting until they are in your barn. When you have spent a good share of your lifetime cultivating a relationship with any four-footed friend, the idea of beginning again is daunting. The advice of other horse owners that "you can always sell it" didn't resonate with me. Animals that came into our lives had always stayed if there was any way we could keep them. No, I had to be sure.

With another horse friend by my side, we drove to the farm and met Raider's Skip. He was a bay roan Quarter Horse, a nice fifteen-hand height with black mane, tail and legs, and absolutely the softest dark brown eyes I had ever seen. His thick mane and tail showed the Spanish heritage of the Quarter Horse breed. And in late spring, he was a dusky light cocoa color. The wonderful thing I was to later learn about roans is that their coat color is always changing. This was one of four different shades he would display over the year. Unfortunately, he also had a reddish brown muzzle and long ears, very mule-like my sidekick teasingly pointed out. I took a short ride down the road, kind of a point and go experience that proved nothing, but something drew me to him. I promised to bring my husband back next time.

The owners told me Raider was the herd leader of the half dozen horses that grazed and stood watching from the dry lot, but a very gentle leader he emphasized. They didn't ride Raider very much, just used him for occasional rides and hauled him a couple of times a year to South Dakota for a big trail ride. They said he was a great horse, but they wanted to invest their time and energy in some younger horses. I thought, maybe it would work if I was brave enough to try. Dick surprisingly cinched the decision. He met Raider the next day, petted him, looked deep into his arched eyes and whispered to me, "If you don't take this horse, you'll always regret it." I was so shocked by such a strong statement coming from my non-committal husband that I blurted out, "We'd like him!" We agreed to a date for a veterinary check and when we might be able to pick him up.

I held my breath watching my veterinarian evaluate my to-be horse. He looked him over carefully, examined his mouth, listened to his heart and lungs and then asked us to trot him back and forth watching for lameness. "He has a kind of cute little dicey trot doesn't he?" my gruff vet asked smiling. I agreed "yes" he did. The only negative finding was very shallow feet which might cause him problems but could be improved with farrier care.

We arrived a couple of days later, trailer in tow with tempting hay hanging inside. Raider wasn't so sure this was such a good idea. He did not like the looks of the ramp leading into that box on wheels; it didn't look like the trailers he had known. But he followed his owner a step at a time up and into the trailer, and stood trembling as he was told it would all be okay and given a final goodbye pat.

At our farm, Raider flew back down the ramp as soon as the tailgate was lowered, glad to be out of that strange smelling thing. We led him into the sand arena, safely separated by fence and electric wire from the curious Lars. We had just taken off his halter when my neighbor drove up and quietly moved in to stand beside me. "I just came to see your new…. buckaroo," she ended as Raider raced by, bucking with each galloping stride around the arena.

I lamented my new ownership woes to a fellow horseperson at work. "I don't know if I should keep him," I began. "He's definitely not what I expected."

Years of trail riding with no arena work left Raider without a clue of what I wanted him to do on the end of the long rope. I just wanted to lunge him in circles around me, but he didn't know circles, just long straight lines. As I attempted to gently pull him in an arc, he braced himself against me and pulled. I could do nothing more than race after him down the long fence line, trying to survive the impromptu "crack the whip" game he had created.

He did know "walk," "trot," and "canter," but he liked to throw a little crow-hop in before the faster gaits.

"So what do you think?" I asked my friend after listing my problems.

"I think it will be fine," she said, then continued, "I always think I've made a terrible mistake for the first month or so after I buy a new horse. But you know, it usually works out fine."

And it did. Raider's sweet gentle nature won us over. He was very smart and eager to please, a perfect combination for training.

He endeared us to him a day at a time until we totally fell in love. His previous owners had told us why he was so special, and we found out how true it all was a little at a time. He licked our hands, savoring the salty flavor and never nipping as he ran his soft pink tongue over any extended palm. If we stood in front of him and raised our chin slightly, he would nuzzle it with his upper lip. His owners had told us that even though they had a nice shelter for Raider, he preferred to be outside in all except the most brutal winter weather. But we learned he actually loved the creature comforts we offered him.

The sand arena became a spa. We would often see him stretched out on his side, loving the warmth of the sun's rays on his skin. The first time we saw him lying there on the late afternoon summer day, we thought he had died and ran calling to him. He raised his head to look at us as if wondering why we were disturbing such a lovely nap. He waited patiently each night to be led into his soft cozy stall with its rubber mat and mounds of fragrant pine bedding, a heated water bucket on freezing nights, and fans to keep him cool and the mosquitos away on sticky summer evenings.

The pear and apple trees, fenced from prying horse teeth, he assumed were planted just for him. He quickly abandoned sweet new spring grass for any fallen fruit that rolled his way. Grooming sessions were heaven to him. He would gladly stand for as long as we were willing to use the shedding comb each spring until his downy brown hair lay around his hooves, or patiently comb tangles from his luxurious mane and tail. The highlight of all grooming was our finding the itchy spots he couldn't scratch. He guided us to each bothersome area stretching his nose into a point and arching his neck as we discovered a new itch, then sighing with relief as we curried and brushed the itch away.

Raider became an instant friend to Lars, who was so happy to be able to play with a younger companion. They were almost inseparable. Every morning began with a race from the barn, up the long run and into one of the pastures for a day of grazing. Raider was like an equine sports car. Built closer to the ground than lanky Lars, he flattened out and ran with his heart, his powerful hindquarters pushing him forward. No matter how hard Lars tried, he couldn't beat his smaller roan buddy. They would while the day away, eating grass or standing with noses pressed to each other's withers, chomping away itches in mutual grooming sessions. They loved being ridden out together, down the gravel road to the Conservation Reserve Program land where we were allowed to ride. We cantered across newly plowed fields in the fall, feeling each stride through the soft rich soil. It was the idyllic picture I had dreamed of—my husband and I both enjoying our world on our two wonderful horses. Perhaps I should have been more alarmed, more cautious of what might lie ahead, understood the fleeting moments we were experiencing.

Dick and I both watched carefully one evening when Raider stepped up into the lean-to and then took turns leading Raider down the barn aisle. We agreed he was definitely lame, noticeably off on one of his front legs. The next day my veterinarian tested each hoof with hoof testers designed to pinpoint sore spots. When we all saw Raider flinch as pressure was applied to a front foot, an abscess was diagnosed.

"Just soak it in warm Epsom salt water 20 minutes, twice a day and he should be fine over time," was the instruction.

Simple thing to do, I thought. Raider was always so calm and easy to handle. But I was wrong. His foot had no sooner felt the warm water than he flew backwards, knocking me to the floor and breaking one of the crossties. So strange, I thought, not like our usually calm boy. We kept trying for more cooperation each time, the only thing to do when a thousand-pound animal must be shown they can stand quietly without fear that something will hurt them. We finally reached an acceptance point, but I was rattled by the experience. Things seemed off; our smooth rounded world now had a rough edge, a crack in normalcy that would grow larger.

The following fall while we were gone on vacation, our caretaker alerted us that Lars seemed to be having trouble going up the short step into our barn for the night. That unsettling alert began a gradual failing of Raider's friend. It seemed such a short time, a brief exhale, and he was gone. We led Raider past Lars to say goodbye, and then Dick and I walked him down the road along the river where we four had traveled together so many times. We didn't want to be there for the burial of our dear friend.

We will never know if it was my canter down the hard packed drive that early spring, the lush spring grass, or the sadness and stress Raider felt at the loss of his companion. The result was the same. We came home from work one evening to find Raider unwilling to move in from the dry lot to his comfy stall. It hurt to watch him try to take a step, shifting his weight from one painful hoof to another.

Once more our veterinarian was there to help us find what was wrong with him, and to guide us in helping our very sore little horse. Raider had foundered. More accurately called laminitis, it meant the inner structure of his feet had been compromised causing heat, blood restriction, inflammation and pain. I knew that in severe cases, foot bones rotate, sometimes finding their way through the bottom of the hoof. Thankfully, X-rays showed very little rotation, but he was hurting. The treatment was once again soaking each foot for at least twenty minutes, but this time in ice cold well water. I was very thankful to have worked through Raider's great aversion to soaking. Every morning and every evening, I put each front foot in a huge black tub and then slowly filled it with water. While Raider munched on a third tub filled with hay, I settled on a bucket in front of him, my back pressed against the cinder blocks of the barn. And we talked.

I told him how much I missed Lars and how sad I knew he was to not have his friend with him. Humans, no matter how hard they try, just couldn't pick up the subtle sign that a oh-so-hard-to-reach spot on the back where the mane ends was itchy or a tail was needed to swish flies off a face. "I'll find another friend for you, Raider," I promised. And I slowly started once again to search for the perfect companion for all of us. A friend found the ad for a five-year-old Quarter Horse/Thoroughbred cross not far from where we lived. "Kind of young," I told her, but the ad stressed that he would be a good husband's horse and anyone could ride him. We did buy Nicsson after several trips to visit and ride him, but luck was not with us this time in our selection. He was not like Lars in temperament as a riding companion or as a new pasture mate for Raider.

Nic proved to be a sensitive and complex boy who often seemed more interested in defeating direction than working in harmony. Raider tolerated the younger horse, but he rarely instigated play sessions with him. Nic had a teasing side that irritated my calm Quarter Horse. He would sometimes toss his head and then strike out at Raider, never connecting or causing harm, but coming oh so close. They grazed side by side but never indulged in the mutual grooming sessions that Raider had enjoyed with Lars.

While Nic and I slowly began working through our own issues, I monitored the progress that my two horses were making adjusting to each other. I thought everything was going better, but then one night when I put Raider's halter on to lead him into his stall, I found him standing with his right eye held tightly shut and tears streaming down his face. He was uncharacteristically nervous walking beside me and barely skimmed past the door frame on his right. He couldn't see out of his right eye.

My veterinarian examined his eye in the dim barn light, searching with his light for pupil contractions and responsiveness. There was no sign of an injury, but reluctantly my mind envisioned Nic's sharp hooves striking out in play. I couldn't imagine how his eye could have been so badly affected in such a short time from any other cause. But the diagnosis was uveitis, commonly known as moon blindness, a progressive disease that can eventually lead to permanent blindness. My veterinarian wasted no time in referring us to an ophthalmologist at the University of Minnesota.

I spent the night before our appointment worrying that we wouldn't succeed in loading Raider into the trailer. He had not been taken anywhere in such a long time, and he couldn't see the trailer on his right side. But he never hesitated when I asked him to follow me up the ramp and into his trailer stall. We placed him on the left side so he could see out the window with his left eye and we entered into a long journey to help him see with both eyes again.

After a few days at the hospital for more testing and a plan of care, we traveled home. My horse could see out of his right eye, but not normally. The University's veterinary department prescribed one medication to help make the pain more tolerable and another to address the disease. The application technique was something Raider would not tolerate. The medication had to be squirted through a syringe into his eye. It was not painful, but he did not like the stream of liquid hitting his eye out of the darkness. Even treats and warm praise didn't help. There had to be another way.

Another trip to the University and a new approach was decided upon. It was a different solution but not necessarily easier, involving implanting a tube which would be used to administer medication into his eye and woven into his mane on the other end. When winter arrived, we had the additional challenge of keeping the liquid from freezing. We first warmed the syringe and then carried it wrapped in heated pads to Raider. Sometimes all went well, but too frequently the liquid would freeze before it reached his eye. We then tried warming it with our hands or the heated pads, and generally we could finally make the apparatus work.

The tube was fragile, indeed, and Nic was always overly curious about anything that was not ordinary. More than once we went to the barn to find the portal device unusable, causing more trips to the university to reattach the tubing which Nic had obviously helped to disengage.

Wanting to give Raider every chance to see again, I found a new way to protect him and his tubing from Nic's inquisitive nose and mouth. It was a Slinky—the clinging Lycra bodysuit designed to keep the coats of show horses smooth, clean and shiny. But why not use one to protect Raider's face and neck? We bought a bright blue one, skintight and shimmering from his shoulder over his face. It zipped tightly closed from under his chin to his chest. Finally, I breathed a sigh of relief that all would be well. That was before I saw the many little horse bite-size holes that altered the Slinky's elegance and exposed tubing once again.

Raider and Nic were not happy about being separated, but there was no other choice. Our pastures and shelters were designed for sharing, not separation, so we rotated the two horses—in the dry lot with the lean-to part of the day, out in the pasture with the pole barn the remainder of the time. Raider was not deeply attached to Nic, but he missed his herd. While Nic raced through a bizarre carnival of bucks and rears and kicks close to the barn, Raider raced around outside the fence, mimicking his brother's antics and adding some of his own. Galloping along the fence parameter, instead of skirting the small drainage pond, he launched himself across the twelve-foot length, never missing a stride.

On one of the repeat visits back to the hospital for more tests, I asked that they also test Raider for insulin resistance since he had experienced a laminitis episode the previous summer. He did show intolerance to sugars which meant the days the horses had always enjoyed grazing the summer away in our shady pastures had to end. The veterinarians advised that Raider not be allowed on grass for more than three hours each day, or that he be fitted with a grazing muzzle to limit his intake of the tasty but dangerous green stuff.

Raider's eye treatment helped until it didn't. We periodically had the pressure in his eye checked by another local veterinarian and our usual vets continued to monitor him closely. Despite the disease, his eye always appeared normal. Then suddenly we saw more irritation in his eye and a change in its shape, and our veterinarian referred us to another eye specialist. This time, the lens in his eye had become dislodged because of mounting pressure. The doctor was able to restore the lens to its normal position but it was a precarious situation. Raider had to remain at rest in his stall to let the eye heal and he was not a cooperative patient. He wanted out and threatened to jump over his exterior half door until we were forced to keep it closed, shutting out the sunlight and outdoors that he loved. When there was no improvement, we reluctantly decided not to try to save his sight any longer. It was fall when he was first diagnosed, now it was spring, and Raider wanted to be a horse.

We opened the doors and the gates and let the horses be together to enjoy pastures once again. Mindful of the hospital's recommendation, we opted for a grazing muzzle for Raider to limit his exposure to grass, but Nic once again changed our plans and complicated our management program. The horses both came trotting in for the night, but there was no muzzle. Nic apparently liked Raider better without one or thought the muzzle was a fun new chew toy. My mental picture of my horses always included them throughout spring, summer, and fall eating green grass surrounded by white fences. It didn't include limited grazing and many hours spent standing in a dry lot eating hay, but that was the new reality of life on our farm.

Throughout Raider's treatment, I continued to handle him regularly and ride him as I always had. I knew that many horses with limited sight, including those that are totally blind, continue to be ridden, even jumping in competition. Raider never reacted to the loss of his eye, though we were careful to make sure he knew when we were on his right side. Unless people looked closely at his face, they rarely realized his right eye was not normal.

One day, a year or two after Raider was diagnosed and recovered from his eye problem, I received a surprising email that confirmed what a wonderful little horse we had decided to make ours. The email was from a woman who was searching for a horse named Raider's Skip and had traced him to us. The horse had belonged to her daughter, and for her thirtieth birthday, she wanted to reunite her daughter with her first horse. We told her that, yes, we had Raider, and they would be more than welcome to come visit him. There are many stories of horses being reunited with a previous owner and recognizing them. Raider greeted his guests with his usual social warmth, snuggling up for pets, and perhaps a treat. While the mother and I visited, the daughter took Raider on a ride. They both looked happy together.

The mother told us what a wonderful horse Raider was. It was a fairy tale of a little girl and her horse, playing hide and seek around hay bales, leaning against him reading a favorite story as he lay flat out on the ground, inviting him up on the porch for a special treat, trusting him to carry her safely and slowly down a steep trail. They sold him because she wanted a jumping horse.

He lived at their friend's home and carried their daughters on trail rides until he was purchased by the owners he had when we found him.

Raider—always loved, always sweet and kind. The little pony every girl should have.

Nicsson—A Change of Circumstance

I watched him dying, my tears falling on his soft red coat, his legs galloping toward somewhere only he could see. Then he was quiet.

Lars was my dream horse. He would have been twenty-one in the spring and I had owned him, trained him, ridden him on trails, and in the show ring from the time I bought him as a seven year old. He and I competed in dressage, and with his wonderful stride and confident manner, we did very well. And now he was gone.

Raider and I missed our big red friend terribly. I couldn't imagine another horse in his stall. I didn't even want to look, the pain was so great. But then one of my horse buddies sent an email about a young Quarter Horse/Thoroughbred for sale near her. I almost deleted her message without really looking. If I were to buy another horse, I wanted one that I could continue to grow with, to build upon what Lars and I had accomplished together. I didn't want a young horse to train. But his owners claimed he was a horse anyone could ride, a husband's horse. Sensible, I thought. "What do you think, Raider?" I asked my Quarter Horse. He looked at me with his great gentle soft eyes and breathed into my open palms. "Okay. I'll take a look," I promised.

We traveled hours back and forth from our farm to meet and watch the beautiful bright chestnut named for his legendary great-grand sire Remnick. Unfortunately, it would be a long time before I learned about the other side of his heritage—a talented, smart, but almost unmanageable, great-grand dam that appeared to imprint most strongly on his personality. As we watched, he moved willingly for his owner, and I was pleased with his quiet responsiveness when I rode him. But sadly, the "magic feeling" telling me I had to own him was missing.

Nic didn't have the soft eye I always watch for, and I was troubled by the many whirls on his face which some say is an indication of a difficult horse. I had reservations. But, his owners attested to his calm disposition on the trail, in shows, as a lesson horse. And there was pressure. I was lonely, Raider was lonely. His owner was selling her farm and he was one of the last remaining horses. He was a beautiful glowing chestnut like Lars, and he seemed kind.

Back on our farm, my husband added to my decision milieu. He reminded me I was getting older. Not something I wanted to hear from my love. And with that in mind, he questioned why I would want a young horse. "Because I need new life in my life," I responded, fighting back threatening tears. I'd just spent almost six months nursing Lars through reoccurring lameness and a terrible sinus infection, only to lose him so suddenly it seemed as though it couldn't have happened. I felt this boy and I could do well together. I was confident of his potential, and so I bought him.

The horse who had stood relaxed in his barn was not the fellow who came to live at my farm days later. "He was really nervous," the student who helped me at the farm commented after helping unload Nic and settle him into his new home. To be expected, I thought. It was his first time away from home with people he didn't know. "Give him some time," my friends advised. So I did. And as October turned into a snowy November, I started riding him and working with him on the ground. He was a little clumsy, stepping on himself and us occasionally, but he was young, just a baby, and his vet check had been good. He was good, but he tested me, pulling back on the line as I lunged him and then racing across the arena in the other direction. I knew that would get better, but our work together came to a halt the first time I rode him down our drive.

He would not go past the stand of pampas grass near the end of our drive. After several attempts and finding no tigers hiding in the wavy shocks, he did hustle sideways past them. The trees and the river were ahead and with each step toward them, his head grew higher and his step more prancing. I tried to calm him, circling him so he would lower his head, but he would not be placated. In his view the landscape was threatening and, at the point where the trees came to meet the road, he froze. "No, I'm not going forward," he said to me. I pushed with my legs and seat, but instead of moving, he threatened to rear. There is nothing good that can come from fighting with a horse in a dangerous situation where it is likely you will lose, so I changed the plan and rode instead around the edge of the plowed field, then back by the sinister grasses several times until he walked quietly past them. We each learned something. He learned to trust himself in deference to my leadership, and I learned that I needed to start training him again on the ground as if he was a brand new student.

I'd been riding and working with horses for over forty years, attended countless clinics, and was coached by many trainers.

Still in the dark, when I couldn't sleep for my daily rehashing of life problems, I had to admit, Nic scared me. He was highly unpredictable in his reaction to the world around him. Heavy machinery operating outside the arena walls did not faze him, yet a flock of birds departing from branches of the old crab apple tree on the way to the barn unhinged him. My talented athlete ducked and pivoted, almost unseating me. A few moments later, he was quiet, lazily walking past the tree and on into the paddock.

There are horse whisperers out there that the universe sends to us to help us on our journey with these beautiful and complicated creatures. I found a trainer and I made good progress with my sensitive guy. We began training extensively on the ground, building my confidence and our partnership. When I began riding out again, we could navigate past the scary tree line with hardly a look. I was relaxing and beginning to really enjoy my new equine partner. All was going well for us.

But one night in mid-winter, although the temperature began at twelve degrees and fell steadily each hour, I decided to brave the cold and work with Nic in the indoor arena. We played on the ground together and then I started to mount him for a ride. As I put my foot in the stirrup and started to climb into the saddle, I slipped, startling my horse. He panicked, whirling around and dragging me, as I lay on the ground, my foot trapped. Then just as suddenly, Nic stopped, the dust settled around us, and my foot slipped freely to the ground. He came to me, running his nose gently down my injured leg. "What have you done to your mom?" I asked. I tried to stand, using a stirrup and then the reins to pull myself up, but the pain was overwhelming. Nic stood quietly by me, unsure what he should do.

I instinctively began calling for help. But banging on the pole barn's tin walls and screaming for help did no good, and I began to think carefully about my situation. Surely my husband would come looking for me soon I reasoned; I just needed to wait. But minutes dragged by and when he did not come to rescue me, I worried that something had happened to him. I was alone and I could freeze if I stayed in the barn. With fear as my motivation, I decided to leave the shelter of the arena and began crawling toward the house. It was a long time before my husband came out to check on us. He found me pulling myself across the snow with Nic watching from the arena, unhappy to be left alone. I couldn't stand, so my husband brought out our low plastic sled from the barn and helped me roll onto it. Shivering from the cold and pain, I insisted my husband put Nic in his stall before pulling me over the frozen ground into the comparatively warm garage where we waited for the ambulance.

My knee had to be reconstructed. I not only could not walk on my leg for many months, I could not lift it on my own. I was terrified I might not be able to walk again. But my surgeon assured me severed nerves would find new pathways, and I would be able to move my leg unassisted by the straps that made lifting it possible. In the living room on the futon couch that was my bed, and then on the exercise mat, I faithfully performed the exercises that would help me walk again with my cats providing companionship and help as only cats can.

I watched the world outside—the ice melting off the porch roof, trees budding, grass changing from brown to green. With spring came my ability to move with a walker and optimism that I would be well again. My physical recovery was very hard, but harder still was acceptance that something that was so much a part of my life might change forever. I'd loved horses since I was a little girl and my father first put me on the bare back of a chestnut Thoroughbred mare. I'd had minor injuries around them, but nothing as catastrophic and potentially life altering as the injury that Nic caused. Tearfully, I faced the truth that I might never fully recover emotionally. There were many cautious steps till I could stand comfortably with my horses again and begin to enjoy them in my space and hours of physical therapy as I learned to walk again.

Over the next six months as the hazy Minnesota summer turned leaves bright green, and the plowed fields around the farm were covered with corn and soybean rows, I began to think about riding again. I hired a young dressage rider to work with Nic. She was talented and Nic's training was going well. I could almost feel him beneath me as I watched her ride and dreamed of the day I would be up there in the saddle. Then during his warm-up one day, Nic stumbled badly, his back legs going out from under him. A veterinary exam found that he had a good deal of pain in his back from the incident and we decided to rest him until he was better. Over the next few weeks, Nic continued to periodically lose control of one or both of his hind legs. My veterinarian suspected neurological damage high in his spine. Or possibly, just as devastating, Equine Protozoa Myeloencephalitis (EPM), a disease transmitted by opossums that could manifest itself in lameness and other catastrophic neurological and physical symptoms. There was no cure and extensive testing would be required to confirm the diagnosis. We could only wait and hope his condition would improve.

The rest of the summer we both recuperated with hand walks or in-hand exercises only. Then late summer and fall came, and another trainer worked with Nic and me on the ground once again, desensitizing him to flapping tarps and bags. I began riding him a little and his pain seemed to be gone. On a bright fall day, the trainer suggested going on a short trail ride, with me riding Raider and her on Nic. She mistakenly didn't warm my boy up first on the lunge line and, as we were beginning to ride up into our hay field, Nic surprised the trainer by jumping a small rivulet throwing her forward in the saddle. He was startled by the sudden weight on his withers and began bucking until he threw her over his head.

The confidence that had been slowly coming back to me

faltered. I continued to ride Nic but more cautiously again. He was an incredible athlete, bred to work cattle, wheeling and charging after them. Just before Thanksgiving, while I was riding in the outside arena, I noticed Nic seemed distracted by something. I followed his gaze but as we rounded the corner, he ducked to the left and pivoted and I flew through the air, landing on my back. I assessed the possible damage and though my back hurt terribly, I climbed back on my naughty horse and worked him for a few more minutes. I tried to treat the event casually, but at dinner when tears fell onto my plate, my husband insisted we go to the emergency room. Eventually, the surgeon found I had fractured two vertebrae in my back. The fragile partnership between Nic and me was put on hold once again.

Time spent on the ground not riding Nic was an education for both of us. Nic was incredibly sensitive, aware of anything new in his environment, and he was very intelligent. He quickly learned new training patterns and remembered them immediately. I worked constantly to keep his mind engaged, to keep one step ahead of him so he wouldn't become bored, to anticipate possible reactions. And he was wonderfully playful—a colt that never really grew up.

If I left his grooming box on the floor before him as I tried to get him to calmly enjoy being curried and brushed, he would select items from it and play with them. He would chew on rubber curry combs and, holding his brush in his teeth, would sweep the concrete barn aisle floor. I outfitted all the windows in the barn with screens to keep the ever-present mosquitoes away and let in cooling night breezes. Unhappily, I gathered the screens with the meshes torn, the frames mangled, from the ground where Nic had dropped them after pulling them from the windows with his teeth. Bars had to be added on all potential horse-contact windows to discourage additional damage. As I painted the wood fence posts near a corner of the barn one pleasant day, Nic tipped over the paint can barely missing covering his hooves in white paint. He followed us around the farm, picking up discarded branches, rooting through loaded manure spreaders, seeking out carefully hidden treats from our pockets. Nic noticed changes in his environment that other horses would not be aware of—a misplaced bucket, a sun pattern that changed from the previous day, a new shadow on the wall. He carefully examined our feet when we wore different shoes and ran his tickling muzzle down our bare legs when we wore shorts. And he was a cuddler, pressing his forehead gently into my chest or wrapping his elegant neck around me and holding me against his side. My horse was a thousand pound playful puppy with the hair trigger response of a rabbit.

Nic was a wonderful patient when he needed medical treatments, taking vaccines like he received them everyday. He stood quietly for farriers and was endlessly patient for saddling and adjustment of training gear. But he would dance in place when I tried to groom him, and all but refused to be led into our drainage basin for a cooling shower. Nic was a chameleon, ever changing from one horse to another, and there was no predicting which horse I would have with me day to day, moment to moment.

When my veterinarian felt Nic had healed enough to work under saddle again, he recommended a western trainer he thought could help us. The trainer rode Nic for several months and then I began riding him under supervision. I was just starting to feel comfortable on my guy again when we finally sold our house and moved from Leap of Faith Farm to our new home in Kansas.

Looking ahead to our lives together, I tried to see us working well in a long developing partnership. But as quickly as the positive image appeared in my mind it faded, and doubt, just under the surface, took its place. As difficult as it had been for me to move past our accident, it may have been just as difficult for him. Knowing in some way he harmed me may have permanently placed a barrier between us, for him just as it had for me—a fear that the scary event might happen again.

I was haunted by a memory of his reaction one day when someone visited our farm, driving their red pickup down near the dry lot where Nic was munching hay. He always checked on visitors but when he heard the pickup, he came galloping to the fence, whinnying excitedly, watching for the driver. It was not who he expected. The driver was not his previous owner, only a stranger. It hurt that Nic seemed to be waiting for someone other than me to find him.

Nic was rarely the quiet calm horse I longed for. Maybe he was just a spirited, playful, and highly sensitive horse or maybe, as tests suggested, he suffered from one or more illnesses that affected his movement and possibly his mind. We tried training techniques, chiropractic treatments, and medication but nothing seemed to help. Well-meaning people suggested that I sell him but if he were to leave me, his future would have been uncertain. Many horses who are healthier than Nic are sent to slaughter every year, and I couldn't bear the thought of that happening to my guy.

A fortune teller once told me Nic and I were meant to come into each other's lives. She said we knew each other and had a relationship in another life. Maybe it is that history that has kept me from letting him go over so many years, made me keep trying to gain his trust and work with him in spite of the veterinarians who had warned me not to ride him. Or maybe it is because it is easy to love the beautiful, smart, athletic horse in my barn.

He was sociable, funny, and seemed to love me. In our years together, we had been through a lot. I am a better horsewoman because of him. I have learned to take things more slowly and to appreciate little steps forward, achieving small goals, because of him. It is not how I imagined our lives together would be. But I still love him, and he is safe. When I had another fall after Nic spooked again, my family begged me to not ride him. Despite their pleas, I did ride him. But in recent years other non-horse related injuries kept me on the ground beside him instead of sitting in a saddle. I kept thinking that I would try someday again, maybe tomorrow.

And at night, oh at night, in my dreams I am astride my beautiful Nic, flying through grass fields, the wind dancing past us as we gallop together into the fading light.

Epilogue:
Return from the Land of Oz

We followed fall winds swirling the leaves of the giant oaks along the drive to Leap of Faith Farm, to our lives there and the beings that were part of it all. But now, another fall almost twenty years later, and it was time to leave. It seemed as though I had been dreaming of returning to my beloved sunflower state forever. There just never was a good time and then the chance of a lifetime had come along with my appointment as Department of Natural Resources Director for Southwest Minnesota and thoughts of moving home had been put aside. But the job had ended and we had begun thinking about the possibility of a move to Kansas .

Without a job, a new life journey was attractive to me, but for Dick, it wasn't a good time for a life change. While I had been immediately secure in my new position, Dick had struggled to find a job that suited his interests and skills. He had completed a degree in Political Science at Minnesota State University in Mankato, but jobs in his field were not plentiful in southern Minnesota. He worked instead as a database manager, first in Albert Lea, an hour's drive away with a tiring commute which sometimes became dangerous when snowstorms made the interstate impassable, and then in New Ulm where my office was located. Eventually, he found his own dream job as a bookseller at Barnes and Noble. Dick has always felt about books the way I felt about horses. The job was ideal for him and close to the farm. Moving to Kansas would mean leaving it all behind.

But we agreed that managing our twenty-acre farm through all of Minnesota's varying weather conditions and with bodies twenty years older than when we arrived was increasingly difficult. My parents were getting older, and they and the rest of my family had wanted us to move home for such a long time, that when they urged us once again to join them, we decided to do just that. We'd sold two houses before buying the farm and it was such a seamless process, listing and selling, that we thought within a few months we would be living in Kansas.

The decision to move seemed simple, the reality of a move was not. A perfect housing market storm emerged on the horizon in 2007 just as we signed the contract with the realtor to list our farm for sale. Prices fell for sellers and options rose for buyers. Our moving plans took almost five years to become a reality. During that time our lives changed drastically.

I missed my position with the state of Minnesota and the people I worked with, but there was much to do to get ready for the move we hoped would soon come. There were repairs to be made at the farm to help us sell, and we kept the house and barn and grounds always in semi-viewing condition. It was a difficult and depressing process.

We contracted with a realty firm in Kansas and another company in Missouri and began jam-packed visits every other month to view houses. I kept a running list of possible homes that would meet our needs—close to family, space for horses, not in town, roads to ride on, one story, easy access for shopping, garden space, trees...it was endless. But it had worked for us before in finding Leap of Faith Farm.

The house viewing trips to Kansas and into Missouri became an arduous venture. Family joined us as we traveled in all directions from a targeted focal spot to tour and evaluate one after another promising homes that were lost because we could not sell our Minnesota farm. The enthusiasm we began with faded as the years went by and our trips became less frequent.

We tried everything to enhance the appeal of Leap of Faith Farm. We advertised in horse publications, put video tours on line, and even turned to the universe for a little help. We buried St. Joseph upside down beneath the peonies along our drive, smudged the house and the barn, and trudged through knee deep snow into the pastures and fields to cast crystal charms upon the land. Nothing worked. And we struggled to maintain a positive attitude. Dick continued to work at Barnes and Noble and I took a part time job with the national Retired and Senior Volunteer Program matching volunteer opportunities with senior volunteers.

When we began our search, we debated how we would transport all our barn and inside kitties to their new home. We looked at giant wire kennels we could put in the back of our SUV's for the trip. How we could safely introduce them all to a new home occupied hours of conversation. And yet, as it turned out, by the time we moved we had lost all but four of our tribe of cats. My horse Lars, that I looked forward to riding and competing with in another state, had died and a new challenging horse that I didn't feel I would ever bond with would join Raider at our new home. The appeal of beautiful riding arenas that we originally looked for on our trips to Kansas lost importance. I endured a terrible riding accident and a second bad fall that would leave me recovering throughout the next several years.

I tried to keep a rhythm to my days keeping true to our pattern of life on a farm. Some time for work, some for creativity, some for play. The years continued on day by day. It seemed there would be no end. We couldn't leave the farm we loved. Then my sister suggested having a phone consult with a fortune teller she had met in the Ozarks that she thought would be helpful. With reservation, I called, and the warm supportive voice assured me there would be changes and within the next six months we would sell our farm and would be living in Kansas.

She told us a family would come and look at our farm. They would not buy it. But shortly after that time, two other families would both be interested and one would make an offer. They would not buy the farm, but they would serve as a catalyst and the next people to visit the farm would buy it. And it happened just that way. We were thrilled to find buyers who seemed to really love the farm and the potential it offered for their four children to explore and play safely away from any roads. But we were disappointed that they had no plans to have horses or use all the wonderful improvements we had made for them.

Under pressure to find a home quickly in Kansas, we pleaded with our realtor, who had grown a little weary of the five-year long search for the perfect place, to dust off her listings and help us once again. We found a slightly less than perfect home in an ideal location, only twenty minutes from the great university town of Lawrence where my sister, my nephew and their families lived, and an easy forty-five minute drive from my parents in Topeka. Although it was not a fixer-upper home, it definitely needed sprucing up after sitting vacant for several years. Yet so many things fit our list that we couldn't say no. My family shook their heads at the barn, filled with decaying hay and doors that creaked back and forth in the winds that whistled through them, and the arena with missing fence, the slanting pipe fence, overgrown rose bushes around the house and the yard with bare and brown patches where green grass should have been growing. But once again I saw the potential in the place—how it would look someday with loving care and time, and with my husband supporting my vision once again, Roaming Wind Farm became ours.

My lifelong dreams and visions came true at Leap of Faith Farm. But after fifty years of roaming, I followed the yellow brick road back from my Land of Oz in Minnesota to Kansas with my husband Dick; my cats—Ghost, Kasota, Dancer and Phantom; and my horses—Raider and Nicsson. And at the end of the rainbow I found where I always wanted to be. There's no place like home.

River Journey

In a Dream
    the ending came
Words flowing from vacant faces
Striking my soul
    with floodwater force

A decade together
    the River and I meandered
Quiet waters—wetlands and lakes
Prairies and woods
    natural fabric of our lives

Symbiotic spirits
    free-flowing
Carving subtle paths—across this land
Blocked by intervention
not of our making

Ghost whisper of prairie grass—heard
    on summer night winds
Above rustle of corn stalks
Across seas of green
    stark brown fields

Farms float as islands on richness of land
    so transformed
That only in grandfathers' memories
Does winged flight of birds
    obscure the sun

Towards these northern plains
    southern spring winds
Carry the warmth of sunflowers
And so—the River and I must follow different channels
    As the currents move us home

A Chronology of Our Friends at Leap of Faith Farm

Our Horses:

Dunny Money—Registered Quarter Horse. Foaled April 21, 1972. Owned May 12, 1975 until his death at Leap of Faith Farm, March 2008

Raider's Skip—Registered Quarter Horse. Foaled May 18, 1990. Purchased May 4, 2002. Lived at Leap of Faith Farm and moved with us to Kansas in November 2012.

Lars (Grand Larsony)—Anglo-Arab/Swedish Warmblood. Purchased as a five-year-old August 19, 1991. Lived at Leap of Faith Farm from 1994 until his death in February 2008.

Nicsson—Quarter Horse/Thoroughbred. Foaled April 2004. Purchased as five-year-old in 2008. Lived at Leap of Faith Farm and moved with us to Kansas in 2012.

Our Cats:

Tasha—Gray long-hair female. Adopted in St. Paul, Minnesota in February 1991; Moved with us to Leap of Faith Farm in 1994 and lived there until her death in August, 2008.

Haley—White and orange female. Adopted as stray young cat in October 1994. Lived with us at Leap of Faith Farm until her death in June 2010.

Dancer—Orange and white male. Adopted as a kitten from our neighbors in November 1998. Dancer lived with us at Leap of Faith Farm and moved with us to Kansas in 2012.

Larena Orange female adult cat. Adopted from our neighbors in 1998. Part of the barn tribe, briefly living as a house cat with us at Leap of Faith Farm until her death in December 2011.

Peaches—White and orange adult cat. Adopted from our neighbors in 1998. Part of the barn tribe at Leap of Faith Farm until her disappearance one Labor Day weekend.

Justin—Yellow young male cat. Adopted from neighbors in 1998. Part of the barn tribe at Leap of Faith Farm until his disappearance.

Chess—Black and white young male cat. Adopted from our neighbors in 1998. Part of the barn tribe and then lived with us at Leap of Faith Farm until his death in 2012.

Jessie—Gray young female cat. Adopted from our neighbors in 1998. Part of the barn tribe at Leap of Faith Farm until her death in 2007.

Kasota—Yellow male cat. Adopted as a stray in 1999. Lived with us at Leap of Faith Farm and moved with us to Kansas in 2012.

Ghost—White female kitten. Adopted as a stray in October 2008. Lived with us at Leap of Faith Farm and moved with us to Kansas in 2012.

Phantom—Brown tabby male adult cat. Adopted as a stray in November 2008. Began as part of the barn tribe. Then lived with us at Leap of Faith Farm and moved with us to Kansas in 2012.

Other Kitties:

Other cats came and went over the twenty years we called Leap of Faith Farm home:

Sage
Cinnamon
April
An unnamed tuxedo
Chloe
Spice

They were ours briefly and then we helped them find their forever homes.

And finally, Wiley—Bantam Rooster. Joined our lives in 1994 and continued to live at Leap of Faith Farm until his death in 2002.

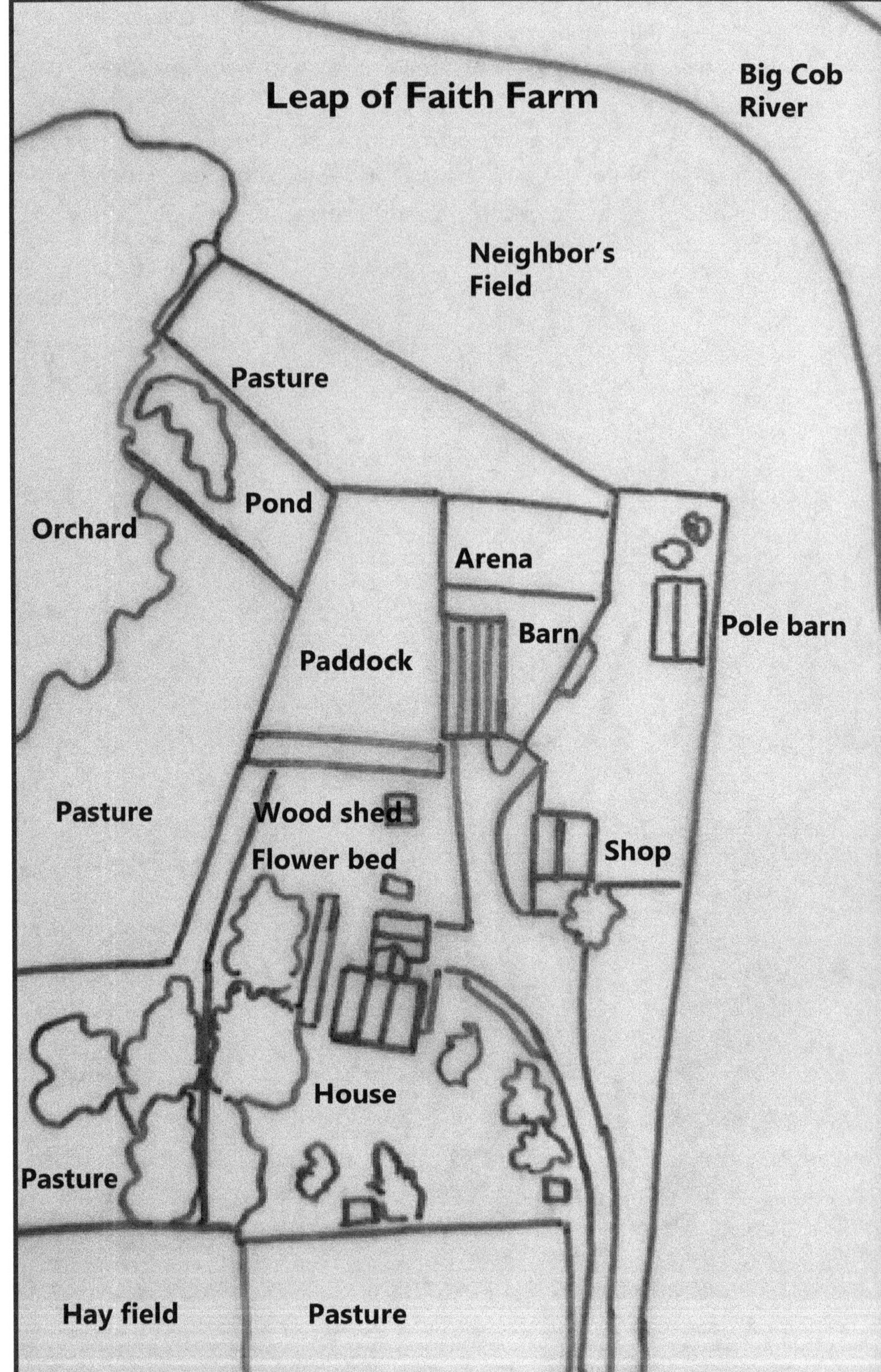
Leap of Faith Farm
Big Cob
River
Neighbor's
Field
Pasture
Pond
Orchard
Arena
Barn
Pole barn
Paddock
Pasture
Wood shed
Flower bed
Shop
House
Pasture
Hay field
Pasture

About The Author

Cheryl Heide lives with her husband, three cats, and two horses on a farm near Baldwin City, Kansas. Her "Roaming Wind Farm" is named for the journey she has made from the time she left Kansas, through the years she spent living in Virginia, Kentucky, and Minnesota, until she finally returned to her home state. The rhythmic flow and lyrical tone of the short stories and poems she has written about the people and animals in her life reflect the love she also has for music and singing. She has published poetry and prose pieces through Guild Press in Robbinsdale, Minnesota, Chicken Soup for the Soul Publishing, Meadowlark Press, several anthologies, and an article in Equus Magazine.

We hope you enjoyed reading Cheryl Suzanne Heide's "AT LEAP OF FAITH FARM." Please order additional print copies from https://anamcara-press.com/ or from your favorite bookseller and leave a review for Cheryl on your favorite bookseller's website!

Other Memoirs To Enjoy From Anamcara Press

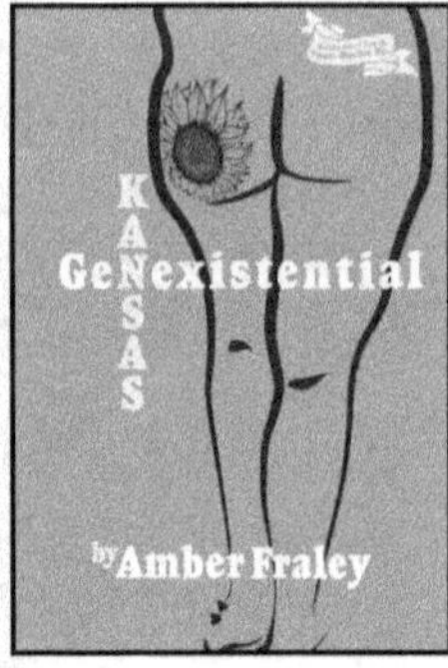

Kansas Genexistential
$21.99

Posts Of A Mid-Century Kid $21.99

Bluebirds to Tikal
$21.99

You Can't Get Rid Of Me
$21.99

Searching for Spencer
$21.99

A Wyoming Cowboy in Hitler's Germany $29.99

Available wherever books are sold and at:
https://anamcara-press.com/

Thank you for being a reader! Anamcara Press publishes select works and brings writers & artists together in collaborations in order to serve community and the planet.
Your comments are always welcome!

Anamcara Press
anamcara-press.com

www.ingramcontent.com/pod-product-compliance
Lightning Source LLC
Chambersburg PA
CBHW070241130726
48053CB00023B/218

* 9 7 8 1 9 6 0 4 6 2 8 4 8 *